MEN FOR GOD

MEN FOR GOD

David Pawson

Anchor Recordings

First published in Great Britain in 2020 by
Anchor Recordings Ltd
Synegis House, 21 Crockhamwell Road,
Woodley, Reading RG5 3LE

**For more of David Pawson's teaching,
including DVDs and CDs, go to
www.davidpawson.com**

**FOR FREE DOWNLOADS
www.davidpawson.org**

**For further information, email
info@davidpawsonministry.org**

ISBN 978-1-913472-20-7

Printed by Ingram

Contents

This book is based on a series of talks. Originating as it does from the spoken word, its style will be found by many readers to be somewhat different from my usual written style. It is hoped that this will not detract from the substance of the biblical teaching found here.

As always, I ask the reader to compare everything I say or write with what is written in the Bible and, if at any point a conflict is found, always to rely upon the clear teaching of scripture.

David Pawson

1

A BURDEN FOR MEN

For about ten years I spoke at conferences under the title "Men for God". In this chapter I will tell you where I got that burden, how I got it and why I did it – because, for the first thirty years of my ministry, every meeting I spoke to was mixed. Then came a time when, whenever I prayed, the one word I kept hearing from God was "men". I shared that with my wife and she said: "You must start talking to men." In fact, she said something else: "From now on you mustn't refuse an invitation to speak to men." It did become too big a burden to answer every invitation. But the burden had taken the previous thirty years to grow and come to fruition.

Some sixty years earlier I had given up smoking. I gave up smoking the day that I took it up and I have never had a cigarette since. Four of us went into the bushes and we smoked a whole boxful and were sick as dogs. I have yet to meet the person who enjoyed their first cigarette but we certainly did not enjoy our first fifty. I was describing that incident in Derby City Hall and the Methodist minister on the platform leapt off his seat and said, "David, I was one of the other three." He had forgotten all about it until that moment. Smoking won't take you to hell, but it will make you smell as if you have already been there. Why did we do it since we didn't enjoy it? The answer is that we wanted to think we were men instead of boys.

Every boy has a kind of picture in his mind of what manhood is, and wants to be that image. It is God's will that a boy should get his image of manhood from his father and that every boy should say, "When I grow up I want to be like my dad." But I meet hundreds, perhaps thousands of men who say, "The last person I wanted to be like was my dad," and many of us react against that image. So we pick up our image of manhood from all kinds of places, and my little image as a boy of nine was smoking. Later, at the age of sixteen, I left school and went to work on a farm because it had always been my ambition to be a farmer and I had spent every holiday on farms. On the farm I got up at four in the morning to milk ninety cows with another man, who had the dubious reputation of being able to swear longer than anyone else without repeating himself. They held competitions for obscenities and blasphemies, and my vocabulary became greatly extended. It is interesting that, once again, this was part of the boyhood image that if you are going to be a man then you have to swear and use bad language. Of course, most swear words come from the two sacred relationships in human life: between man and woman, and between man and God. They take these relationships and profane them. That is what swearing does; it is degrading something that is good – something that is even holy. So I grew up with an image of manhood that I picked up from all over the place.

A year after I went farming I met a man called Jesus who I thought had been dead for two thousand years, and it was a bit of a shock to find he hadn't been. I went back to the farm and found myself singing choruses to the cows at five o'clock in the morning. That was a minor miracle, because you don't feel like singing normally at that time in the morning when you face that kind of task. I wish I had taken out a patent for it because years later, in *Farmers Weekly*, I discovered an article that said music helps milk flow in the cows. At that stage many farmers used to pipe music into the cowshed to improve milk flow. I can claim to have discovered that long before it was publicised.

Then life began to change quite radically. I began to preach – not in churches, they would not have had me then – but I would preach anywhere I could, and my pulpit was an ex-US Army Jeep left over from World War II. I would park it anywhere there were people. There was a queue outside, down at the beach at a place called Whitley Bay, Northumberland. Anywhere I parked the Jeep I would preach. I wanted to tell the world what I discovered – Jesus is alive, and that has changed the whole of history. I was so excited that, naively, I just got up anywhere and preached about it. Soon, about seventy or eighty young people had joined me and we were quite a gang in the northeast of England. We became well known there, and we went anywhere.

Later, I found myself preaching in churches. This is how it happened. I went to have tea one Sunday afternoon with a converted bookmaker from Durham, and I knew he was preaching that night in a chapel in a place called Spennymoor. I went with him to hear him. On the bus there I said, "What are you preaching about tonight, Jack?"

He replied, "I'm not preaching tonight, you are."

I got up in the pulpit and managed to get out my whole theology and my whole testimony and everything else in seven minutes flat—a feat I have never achieved since. So now there was a tension in my life. I loved farming and I wanted to be a farmer, but now I found myself loving preaching and wanting to be a preacher.

I want to share with you now a simple secret that I have worked out about this matter of guidance. Some people seem to make such a meal of getting guidance from the Lord. My arrangement with him is this: "You're the Lord, therefore you're my boss. It is not my job to try and read your mind. It is your responsibility to tell me what you want me to do." I made a solemn promise to him years ago: "If you will tell me clearly what you want me to do, I'll do it. If you tell me something to say or somewhere to go, provided you tell me clearly, I'll be obedient." I think that by his grace I have managed to keep that promise through the years. Though it has had its costs and consequences, nevertheless it means I don't search for guidance. If I don't hear anything from him, I assume he wants me to carry on doing what I was already doing. But if he wants me to do something else, he knows he has only got to tell me clearly. Now that saves an awful lot of hassle, and that is my approach to guidance for what it is worth. I can only say it works, though not always in the way you want it to.

So, one morning I got up and said, "Lord, will you please tell me by twelve noon today whether you want me to be a preacher or a farmer." At ten-thirty, I was having coffee with a friend on the farm and he looked straight up at me and said: "David, you will finish up in a pulpit, not behind a plough."

I said, "That's not clear enough Lord," and I left him, went out into the road and I bumped straight into a retired Methodist minister. I had not seen him for years. I had known him when I was a little boy and I said, "Hello, Mr Scott, how are you?"

He did not tell me, but when you say "How are you?" you do not always expect an answer." He said: "David, why aren't you in the ministry?" It was now eleven-thirty and I said, "That's clear enough, Lord." While I stayed on farming for another three years and took a degree in agriculture at Newcastle University, nevertheless I knew that my future was clear.

Just a few weeks later my father said, "I want to talk with you." I wondered what I had done wrong but he said, "I know you want to be a farmer, and I have arranged for a little farm in Scotland for you to rent as soon as you have reached twenty-one." I had to tell him that he was just a few weeks too late, and my heavenly Father had got in first. That was quite something, and when I drive past the little farm I often look at it and wonder if I might still be milking cows there – and I would love to. Put me on a tractor ploughing on a nice day, with seagulls flying around, and I am as happy as the day is long. But it meant something different, and so in 1950 I offered to become a Methodist minister.

I had never been in any other denomination. I did not even know any other, but in fact my forefathers had been Methodists right back to the time of John Wesley. One of the first of the preachers in the family was John Pawson, a Yorkshire farmer and a direct ancestor of mine. Since then, everybody had either been farmers or preachers – or both. There was a family tradition, but now this was not a tradition, it was my own decision and my life. So I offered to the Methodist church for their ministry, and they said, "Well, we can't accept you for another year."

I responded, "I'll go anywhere you send me for a year and do anything you tell me for a year."

So they said "Right."

I said: "Within the British Isles."

So they replied: "Right, you can go to the Shetland Islands" which was about as far away as they could get me – and which I had always thought from the school atlas were in a box! I set sail from Leith, the port in Edinburgh, in a coal-fired ship. We passed Aberdeen and we passed John O'Groats. Then we passed the Orkneys. So we went on and I thought, "Where are we? Is this the Shetland Islands?" Finally, we finished up there, where I looked after five churches and had a motor boat to travel between them.

It was a wonderful experience, but the first funeral I had, was I think the beginning of the burden which I began sharing in 1950. It was the first funeral of a man, and back then no women came to the funeral, only men. For the first time, the church was crowded with men. Every Sunday it was a lifeboat church – meaning "women and children first". Now, for the first time, here was a church packed with men, which surprised me a little, and then we got to the cemetery. At the cemetery I went through the routine or the ritual and walked away from the grave, but after I walked away the men stayed there and did something else. I did not quite spot what they did so I made inquiries. Apparently it was a freemason who had died and all the lodge turned up for the funeral and were doing something to say goodbye to the mason whom we had just buried. I knew nothing about freemasonry at that point but I inquired, asking, "Why are you all freemasons? Why are you all in a lodge?" Because none of them came to church and they began to tell me why they had joined. The main reason, I discovered, was that, after World War II, they had come home and had missed all the male company so much. They looked around for a place where they could be "one of the lads" again and found the lodge, and all the ex-forces men had joined up. They told me what fellowship they got, and what brotherhood it was, and all the rest of it. They even said, "You should join; we'll put you up if you're interested." I nearly did. I am very thankful that I didn't because I know much more about it now. They told me it would help me in my career, which I found a little strange. I have since discovered there are churches in London that would not have you as their minister unless you were "on the square". I am glad now that I did not join. I have since discovered that it is a dangerous way for men to find brotherhood and fellowship. In fact, some people wrote a little booklet about me which they circulated, warning people against this dreadful man David Pawson.

I have seen the fruits of some of these things. I was in a sports stadium and an elderly couple came up to me after the meeting. He was a tall, soldierly looking man. I would put them in their seventies, but she was in quite a bad state. She was bent over, she was shaking, her cheeks were sunken and she looked quite ill. The husband said to me "Will you pray for my wife? She's been such a good wife to me for so many years but I can't bear to see her like this."

I replied, "Well, I don't like to pray for healing until I know what is wrong. What's wrong with her?"

He said, "That's the problem, the doctors can't find out."

I responded, "Well, I don't like to pray until I know what I am praying about, so I will ask the Lord to tell me, and if he does we will go ahead."

I asked the Lord and he did. I said to the man, "Are you a freemason?"

He said, "Yes – I don't go to the lodge much these days but yes I am."

I said "In the name of Jesus, go home, burn everything you've got connected with that, and your wife will be healed."

He replied, "I don't know where everything is," and the wife said, "I do."

Wives tend to be like that. It is quite irritating. If you ever lose anything, go to your wife and she will ask where you last had it, and there it is.

Anyway, they went home and they had the bonfire and she was no better. They burned things in the back yard and there was no improvement. He actually shouted up to the sky and said, "God, that man said she'd be healed if we burned it and we burned it, and she's no better."

For the first time in that man's life, God spoke to him and he said: "There is more in the garage."

They went to the garage and found some other stuff and put it on the bonfire, came back the next night, came to me after the meeting, and I could not believe my eyes. The wife looked ten years younger. The husband looked as if I had given them a million pounds!

There was a boy of fourteen who lived near us. He was a bed wetter and could not go camping without taking a rubber sheet, which caused all sorts of taunting and teasing. The parents had him to doctors, a psychiatrist and everything, and they could not cure this bed wetting. A friend of mine went to tea there and said, "Is there freemasonry in this family?"

"Yes, his grandfather's the grandmaster of the lodge."

My friend simply prayed about that, and the boy has not wet the bed once since. Now you can explain these things away if you wish, but a man came to me not long ago, a medical doctor, and he was shaking with fear as he sat in the chair. I said "What's the matter?"

He said, "I've just been inducted into the thirty-third degree. I found out that worship was to Lucifer. I go to church and I am scared stiff." Well, we got that sorted out.

I was once in Douglas, Isle of Man, and preaching in the theatre there. One day, a man came up to me on the promenade and asked, "Are you David Pawson?"

"Yes," I replied.

He said: "Are you the man who says you can't be a Christian and a freemason?" I confirmed that and he said: "Well, I'm both. I'll give you two minutes to prove to me that you can't be both, and if you can prove it to me in two minutes, I'll resign."

What a lovely challenge! I remember taking my watch off and saying: "I'm not going to talk to you about the thirty-third degree and what you get up to at the top, I am going to talk to you about one of the first oaths you took, one of the first promises you made: a bloody oath about what you would do to anybody who betrayed the secrets. Jesus said that if you even wish anybody dead you had begun to be a murderer. How about taking a bloody oath like that?" He opened his mouth to say something and I said, "I know what you are going to say. You are going to say it is only words, it is only a bit of ritual – we don't mean it. In the same Sermon on the Mount Jesus said "Let your 'yes' be 'yes' and let your 'no' be 'no', always meaning what you say." That is a little neglected bit of the law of Christ that Christians don't always remember, but it is there.

I continued, "If you meant that oath, you were going against the Sermon on the Mount; if you didn't mean it, you were going against the Sermon on the Mount – and you say you are a follower of Jesus."

Well, I have to say he resigned that afternoon and I did it in a minute and a half. It would cost him a lot because the Isle of Man is riddled with it, where tax exiles go and some do their commerce in the lodge. It was going to cost him a lot in his business but he resigned.

We are talking about serious things. I want to see in the church a brotherhood of men which beats that – that has no secrets, that is in the light, and where the name of Jesus is central. That is what Jesus meant the church to be, a brotherhood. That is why he chose twelve men to start it. It is amazing that we go for the women and children today whereas Jesus, to build his church, went for men, working men, most of whom worked with their hands. There was only one pen pusher among them. Jesus chose twelve ordinary working men and started a church that when I first spoke on this numbered fifteen hundred million. When will we learn to do it Jesus' way? What I hope is that in every church there will begin a men's discipling programme.

It worries me when I go to church after church and say: let me see your programme of activities. It is usually an awfully long list, with things for babies, for play groups, for the youth, for pensioners, for women's coffee mornings. I look in vain in nine churches out of ten for anything for men, yet that was how Jesus began.

I discovered that most churches have more women than men. In the last two parish churches I preached in there were five women to one man, and he looked as if he had been dragged there. The average of churches I have been in is two and a half to one. I don't mean there is half a woman there, but that five to two is the average. There are some that are a little better, but why is it that the church is so lacking in men.

I have always been someone who wanted to know *why*. I began it as a little boy and my parents got fed up with me, "Why daddy?"; "Why mummy?" I have never stopped being like that. I want to know why things are the way they are, and I began to ask why it is that the churches seem so like that. Remember that in the Old Testament, when God wanted to find out the strengths of the people of Israel, he said: "Count the men over twenty who are able to fight." I use that as a rough and ready gauge. I was invited to go into churches and look at them and see them as, hopefully, the Lord sees them, and give them some counsel and advice. One of the first things I do is count the men over twenty who are fit to fight the battles of the Lord. That gives you a very good idea as to the real strength.

I make no apology for saying that I believe the strength of any church is in its men. That is why I have been concentrating on that. So why is there this lack? From the Shetlands I went to college and studied theology in Cambridge. There I nearly lost my faith. I certainly lost my faith in the Bible, but I did not lose my faith in God. They taught us to read the Bible with a pair of scissors and cut it up and cut things out, but anyway I managed to hold on to my faith and came back out – but again into these churches where it was largely women and children. Why?

Actually, the Methodist church told me that they wanted me to be an evangelist. They gave me a caravan and a mobile van to pull it, and sent me off to Yorkshire. It was still pretty tough up there. I went down into the pits and into the pubs and clubs and tried to evangelise, and some came to the Lord. But after a year I knew that I was not an evangelist. It is great to find out what you are not. Then you stop trying to be what you are not. Find out what God wants you to be and go after that, but do not try to be what he does not want you to be. That is a killer, and I meet too many Christians trying to do what God has given somebody else a job to do. I knew that I am not an evangelist. Mind you, I do not regret that year. I learnt a great deal about myself, we did see conversions, and I got a wife out of it. So it was not wasted.

I was coming back to the caravan at the end of the year and said, "Lord, I am sure you don't want me to continue in this. I'm sure you've got something else for me, but it's been a wonderful learning experience; thank you for it, but what do you want me to do?"

He said clearly, "There will be a letter waiting in the caravan for you." I couldn't wait to get there. I got to the caravan, opened the door and there was one blue envelope on the floor. So, I picked it up feverishly and opened it and had to sit down. At the top of the letter was the Royal Air Force crest, "We are looking for a chaplain in the Royal Air Force. Nine men have applied for the vacancy but we wanted to add your name to the list of interviewees – are you willing?" I searched the caravan to see if there was another envelope somewhere, but there wasn't, so I had to assume this was what God wanted me to do. I had never been in the forces. There was still conscription in those days, to National Service, but if you were on a farm you were exempt – food was more important than guns immediately after the war. So I had never been called up and did not want to be.

Anyway, I went to London and was interviewed. I will never forget that interview. It was a big room with a long table covered with a green cloth, and behind it sat officers of the Royal Navy, Army and Royal Air Force, in uniform, and there was one single chair in front of that table. I took one look through the door and thought, "I'm not going in there." I shall always be grateful to the sergeant who was on duty at the door to see us in, one by one. As I passed him, he said, "Imagine the men in their underwear, sir." I went in and I "saw" them all in string vests and lost all my fear of them. I relaxed, I enjoyed it, and they gave me the job. They said: "Go immediately to the Central Medical Establishment (CME) in Holborn and have a medical. I found myself going through a medical with aircrew. I recall going into a room stark naked, and there was a doctor in a white coat sitting behind a desk. He looked up and said, "Ah, Padre, come on in." I have been trying to figure that out ever since – I thought: "Do I have a trademark around me? I happened to tell one of the other men having a medical what the doctor had said, and he replied, "At least he didn't say 'Come on in, Rabbi.'"

I went into another room and there was a man saying, "Now I need to test your hearing. Repeat every word I say: 'Fish' and I said 'fish'; 'chips', and I said 'chips'; '*&%$'." I said, "Look I'm going to be a chaplain – I can't say words like that."

He said "You're in", and he signed.

I found myself facing a congregation of hundreds of men. I had all my old sermons in my pocket and they went off like a lead balloon! I realised that I had been adapting myself to preaching to women and children, and most preachers in this country have done the same. It is quite different talking to men. They want it straight from the shoulder. They don't want it dressed up in nice language. Even if they disagree with you, they want to know what you are really saying. "Come on out with it!" I had to throw my sermons away and that three years in the RAF as a chaplain did wonders for me.

Unfortunately, it has made me a little too blunt in speech, and I find that civilian churches tend to react against that from time to time. I have discovered that they do not like outspoken preachers, so I am usually introduced as "no stranger to controversy". All that means is that I tell it as it is, and I speak it out, and I have found that is what men want even if they come and disagree with you about it. I came back into civilian life determined that any church I was pastoring would have as many men as women in it, and that means asking why are they not there.

I came up with a number of reasons: Number one: two world wars robbed the churches of men. They went away to the war and they did not come back. I don't mean those who died, I mean those who lived but did not come back to church. They had seen things and done things that were quite incompatible with faith and a good God. They said: "How can I believe in a good God after the murder and blood of the trenches of World War I?" I was in a church in East London where before World War I they had a men's meeting on a Monday night of a thousand men. They influenced national politics. One speaker at the meeting called for the resignation of a Cabinet Minister. There were Members of Parliament present; that meeting spoke to the nation and was effective. I asked the church whether they still had that meeting now. "No," came the reply.

"When did it go?"

"We tried to revive it after World War I. We got up to about twenty or thirty and then it fizzled out."

That could be said of many churches. If you look at the war memorials in churches, have you noticed how many more names there are from World War I than World War II? There had been a drop and World War II simply accelerated it. It meant that World War I led to a gigantic social revolution in England that had never happened before. Never before had so many men gone to war. Of course it was voluntary at first, later conscription came.

Therefore, for the first time, women were taking over men's responsibilities. The home was run by the women for four years in some cases. The factories were now full of women; the factory hands were female. It is no accident of course that they immediately demanded the vote at the same time. "We are doing a man's job." Only men had been able to vote up until then. Now I am not saying this was a good or bad development. What I am trying to communicate is that a gigantic social revolution had taken place in the absence of the men, and we have not recovered from that. When the men came home exhausted from the war, they virtually said to their wives: "You are doing a grand job, you just carry on." From that day, most of the decisions in most homes in England are made by the wife and not the husband. The husband regards his responsibility as fulfilled when he brings the wages home. That is his bit done. The wife has to make the major decisions, and in many homes it is the wife who has to budget the way the wages are spent, whereas the Bible puts that responsibility firmly on the man. Wives should not have to worry about money.

It is the man's responsibility to make adequate provision and to budget, but in many homes I go to, the poor wife is struggling to balance payments on the television, the car, the housekeeping and everything else. That is a burden she should not be carrying, but in most homes she is the queen so she rules, she reigns.

That was World War I and we had many years to make up for, to get the men back to church, and it was an uphill battle, not easy.

A second reason, and I am speaking plainly, is some effeminate clergy. The selection process has gone for safe rather than risky people, and one of the characteristics of masculinity is the willingness to take risks and to stick your neck out. Of course that is always a threat to a system. There is also the fact that ministering to women and children for most of the time affects a person. I was sitting in a family service with my wife. I am going to caricature so that you recognise that this is nearly what happened. The man preaching said: "Now can anyone tell me anything about a man called Daniel?"

There was dead silence in the congregation. Nobody answered and a little housewife in the front row, with a row of babies in pushchairs in front of her (I don't know if they were all hers or not), raised her hand and said, "I think I know."

The clergyman said, "Yes, what do you know about Daniel?"

She replied, "He pulled a thorn out of a lion's paw." That is an old Greek legend. She had tried and the priest said, "Not quite right, but good try; anybody else?"

"Nobody else. Well I will have to tell you: Daniel was thrown into a fiery furnace." My wife dug me in the ribs and just whispered, "The blind leading the blind," and we began to giggle.

I looked around at the men at that point and they were either checking to see that they had the same colour socks on or they were studying the electric light fittings. They were thoroughly embarrassed. It was supposed to be a family service but there was nothing for men in it. The sermon was treating us all like a Sunday school class, and those men looked as if they couldn't wait to get out. They were totally out of their setting and context.

The clergy produces the church. The one problem with being a minister or a vicar or a pastor is that people follow you. Of course you say you want that, but actually they don't follow what you say, they follow what you do and what you are.

A third reason is that it is much easier for women to become Christians than men, and I want to explain why. Every woman, in her heart, is looking for a man to whom she can entrust her life, someone she can trust to protect her, to provide for her, to do what she needs – someone to look up to, to honour and obey. Of course, when they find Jesus they have found the perfect man. It is almost natural for them to respond to Jesus, especially if a woman is in a bad marriage or is a single mother. They respond so readily to finding a man whom they can trust. Men are rather different. We have a cast-iron muscle in the back of our necks. We like to be independent. We do not want to admit we need help from anybody – we will battle through, even if it kills us.

Our independence is part of our masculinity and so to become a Christian a man has to do two things which are against his nature. First he has got to come and accept Jesus because he needs him. The man's instinct says: "I don't need any help, I can manage my own life." A man said to a friend of mine, "Do you expect me to come before the Lord with open hands and arms and confess my life's a failure and I can't manage without him – I'm damned if I will." You can guess what my friend said to him quietly: "You will be damned if you don't." Which is the truth, but he was expressing this male independence, and especially between twenty and forty-five – provided we have got our health and strength – we can manage our own life. We don't need anybody to tell us what we should be doing, unless a major disaster comes. Unless someone is found out in crime and then becomes a Christian; it takes a disaster, poor health, a failed business, a business partner who has run off with the funds, a broken marriage.... Between the ages of twenty and forty-five it usually takes a pretty big disaster to tell a man he needs help. Then, once he has trusted Christ, and in a sense taken a "feminine" part towards Christ, he is now part of the Bride of Christ, looking to Christ as his "husband". He then has to do another somersault against his nature and remain a masculine man.

Too many Christian men surrendering to Christ become wimps. In relationship to Christ a man must become more "feminine"; in relationship to other people he needs to remain "masculine" – towards his family, towards his colleagues, towards everybody else. Now, that is quite an adjustment, a double somersault, and it is only the grace of God that can help him do it. Too many men have lost their manhood when they became Christians, and that is a tragedy.

Let me illustrate this. I went to south Wales. A woman came up to me after the meeting and said: "Mr Pawson, I have got a problem, will you help me with it?"

I said, "Have you got a husband as well as a problem?"

"Yes."

"Is your husband the problem?"

"No," she replied.

Then I asked, "Have you been to your husband with the problem."

"No."

"Why not?"

"It's a spiritual problem and he's not a Christian."

"What difference does that make?"

She said, "Don't you understand? He hasn't the first understanding of spiritual things and this is a spiritual problem."

I said, "But your husband is the man that God wants you to go to with it."

She said, "I can't believe that."

I replied, "God wants to answer your problem through your husband. That's why he gave you your husband."

"Well, I just can't believe it," she said again.

I said "Listen, God once spoke to a man through his

donkey, and you are saying that God can't speak through your husband."

Now that convinces nine out of ten women, which tells me what they think of their husbands. But she was not convinced and she went away and spread rumours all over the place: "Don't go to David Pawson with a spiritual problem. He doesn't understand what it is like being married to an unbeliever." She did a lot of damage to my reputation.

Nevertheless, a year later I was in the same place and she was there again, and she said, "I've got another problem Mr Pawson, and this time it is my husband. So I can't go to him with it."

So I asked, "What is your problem this time?"

She said, "What do you do with a husband who's way ahead of you spiritually?"

"What do you mean?"

She said "Well I was angry with you for a couple of months because you wouldn't help me and I tried to get help elsewhere and nobody would help me. In desperation I said to my husband: 'Could you help me with my problem?' and he gave me the answer. I don't know who was more surprised, him or me. From that day he began to be interested in spiritual things. Now he is a Christian and I can't keep up with him—he is so keen and so enthusiastic, he's way up here and I can't cope."

I said to her, "You know your problem – you wanted your husband just where you were. Well, it's your job as wife to be where he is. He is your head."

You see, I believe that a Christian wife should still regard her unbelieving husband as her spiritual head. But wives usually come to Christ before husbands, and that creates a problem. It can break a marriage up.

A lady came to Christ in one village and the vicar was so excited he had her giving testimonies at meetings and all over the place – his first "trophy", you know. A husband in the pub was telling people, "Jesus ran off with my wife." Any wife who becomes a Christian first needs to be told very quickly: "Don't preach; don't spend all your days in church." The Bible says you have got to win your husband without a word by becoming more attractive to look at and more attractive to live with, and when your husband feels he has got a better wife with Jesus, he is going to get interested. (That is 1 Peter 3 if you are interested. The Bible is very practical.)

It is the easiest thing for children to be brought to faith in Christ. If you love them and they trust you, it is so easy to get a child to talk to Jesus. Wives, women generally, are the second easiest. Men are the toughest. That is why the church has concentrated on summer schools and women's meetings. But Jesus started with men. I believe we should really re-learn to do it his way, and if I had all my time over again my first priority as a pastor of a church would be to disciple men. All other things would become secondary to that.

If you get the men, the women and children will follow. If you get the women and children you can drive the men further and further away. If his wife has become a spiritual racehorse while he is still at the starting post, you are driving a wedge in that marriage. I have told more than one wife when she has asked me: "What can I do to get my husband saved" – "Stop going to church."

They always reply, "No, seriously, what should I do?" I then say that I was serious, and in so many cases it has worked. The wife has found it so easy to give her life to Jesus, whatever kind of a husband she has; the husband finds it more difficult to sense his need.

Now these are some of the reasons that gave me a burden for men. But I was also developing the same burden for men by what was developing out there in society. While I have been in the ministry there has been a gender revolution. It began in the 1960s with something called "unisex". I remember, years ago, I was going to Singapore and therefore I needed to get my hair cut first. There was a law in Singapore against men's hair touching their collar. It is the way they dealt with anti-social elements in their city, and so (since my hair was touching my collar) I had to go and get it cut. I told my wife that I was going into town and she said, "I have got to go in too, can I come with you?" So we parked the car and went our separate ways and I found (in those days) a hairdresser that did not need appointments and I walked in. As I did so I noticed this word "unisex" and inside I found both young men and young women doing the hairdressing and men and women clients. So I sat down and an extremely attractive young lady started cutting my hair – a new experience for me, not unpleasant. I was chatting away and I looked in the mirror and saw on the other side of the room my wife with a young, smart handsome Italian cutting her hair. Neither of us had known we were going to the same place and we just saw each other – we exploded and roared with laughter. I don't know what the staff saw, but it seemed so ludicrous. It was the thin end of a wedge. Men began to have their hair much longer. Women began to cut it shorter. Men began to wear earrings and jewellery and carry handbags. Women began to wear jeans and jackboots. There was confusion.

That was the beginning of a confusion between male and female, which has accelerated ever since. Now we do not know where we are. I believe behind it was not just a social trend. I believe Satan, whose other name is Apollyon the destroyer, and who cannot create anything, finds his joy in destroying what God has created. He is the original vandal. I believe Satan is destroying male and female, quite deliberately, because God put chivalry in romance. Chivalry has now been labelled chauvinism. I have been rebuked for letting a lady go through the door first. Our whole sense of values about gender has been distorted. Now let me say something about the trend we call "feminism". There is a legitimate complaint behind it: that women have been treated as second class citizens and of unequal value to men. That is the right complaint and we need to hear it as men because we have all been guilty of it in some way or another. However, the solution proposed is the wrong solution. That is to obliterate all differences, call us all "persons" and become "politically correct".

"Politically correct" is far from being biblically correct and there is an increase in tension here. There are Christians who are more concerned with being politically correct than morally correct. Let me trace the development further; in the 1970s the age of "homosex" – it came out of the closet. It is now legal and what becomes legal becomes "all right". When anything is recognised legally it is accepted by the population as "right". That has implications for legalising drugs, legalising prostitution and many other political causes.

We are reaping a harvest today of all this which will go on and get worse and worse. Until men are true fathers, heads of their house and leading their wives and families (not dictating to them, but leading them) we are going to have an increase in perversion and the Bible does call it that. It is an abomination to God, he never intended it, he did not build our bodies for it. That passage is too delicate to be used for that. That is what is happening.

The bisexual and transsexual were the next stage in the process. I remember one day my secretary, a lovely lady, always cool, calm and collected, came into my office in hysterics and I said, "Whatever is the matter?"

She finally said, "There is somebody waiting to see you and I just can't cope."

So I went through to the outer office and there was a middle-aged woman with a hat and coat and a handbag sitting in a chair. I sat down beside her and said, "What's the trouble, dear?"

She replied, "I'm so worried about my wife and children." I did a kind of double take; we had three psychiatrists in the church and I wondered if one of them might be free to give me a hand.

Then I realised this person was perfectly sane. I noticed the hands were twice the size of mine, great big tough hands. So I said, "I think you'd better tell me."

"I was a gunner in the Royal Navy."

I could see the hands.

"I came out of the Navy and couldn't stand life at home with the wife and kids and ran away to London and got into bad company and got into kinky sex and began to dress as a woman. Finally, I had the operation, penis removed, hormone treatment, and am now a woman." This person became so depressed and went to the River Thames and was ready to jump in, but met an evangelist who walks up and down the Embankment stopping suicides and giving them gospel tracts. He stopped this person, gave them a tract, made them say the sinner's prayer, and then gave the name and address of someone who would help them – and gave them my name and address!

This was actually back in the early seventies, and it was the first time I had a pastoral situation like that. I looked at all my books on counselling and not one of them mentioned this. I thought of all my training at Cambridge and it had never come within a million miles of telling me how to handle this. It took six months to get that person straight. I had to say: you must not go back to your wife and children. That is just going to confuse them further.

Finding a job for that person was almost impossible. I

went around employer after employer, begging them to take this person on, but when they found out that he was a person using the women's toilet but with a man's mind and memory, they did not want to know. Finally, I got a Christian employer to take them on – gradually, and slowly but surely.

Have you ever thought about how to help a person to realise who they are in Christ when they have already had an irreversible sex change? Think about it. How do they discover what God intended them to be? That was the first, but I am afraid it was far from the last. I was later told that there are tens of thousands more such cases in England.

You can get it free on the National Health Service, and they have even done a series of television programmes on how to do it. I was talking to a couple at a cocktail party in London. I said, "What are your jobs?"

The man said, "I'm a surgeon and my wife's a psychologist."

I responded, "Oh you look after body and soul?" as a kind of joke.

They said, "That's just what we do. We have our own private clinic."

I asked, "What kind of people come there?"

"Oh, people who want to change sex. I change their bodies and my wife changes their minds."

"Do you have many customers?" I asked.

"We've got a waiting list of hundreds."

We are living in a funny world, in which people don't want to accept what God has made them, a world in which they want to say: "I will choose what I want to be."

Most of the men I have counselled, and some I have managed to persuade not to go ahead with it, have been men who wanted to be looked after rather than have the responsibility of looking after anyone else. That is what I have discovered. They want to be a woman and have a man to look after them rather than face up to the responsibilities of being a man under God. Well, that has been society's trend and this gave me a burden to help men to be men before God, to be what God meant them to be. Not that I count myself a model for manhood.

So, we have many women now in men's spheres. This is one of the biggest changes. Women now use guns and drop bombs. Now it is normal for women to kill. It is only a few years since the British forces ceased to put men only in the fighting line. That is a gigantic change and our grandfathers would have been absolutely astonished at the development. Boxing, wrestling – women want to do everything men can do. A woman champion arm wrestler in an Australian newspaper really attacked me for speaking against feminism.

We are still not at the end of the trend. It was Oscar Wilde who was asked by a lady at dinner, "What is the essential difference between you as a man and me as a woman?"

He said, "Madam, I cannot conceive," which was a typical Oscar Wilde cliché.

The possibility now is that families will be completely indifferent to gender. I mean that you could be living with your wife and children in a house, and in the house next door, both parents and all children are female and in the house next door on the other side both parents and all children are male. We are not talking about science fiction. There is an all-female family in Britain which has used artificial insemination. With the ability to find out early in pregnancy the gender of the foetus, you can choose now, and many parents I fear are choosing abortion because the foetus is not the sex they wanted. That is happening. What is happening to God's intention to create male and female?

Finally let me add that the confusion has now got right inside the church, and that is my biggest burden. It is one thing for society to rebel against God's ordering of our lives – but for the church to join in! The church means Christian men to me, and they ought to be leading society uphill rather than following society downhill. It seems to me that the church follows the world, only fifteen years later, so we get a reputation for being old-fashioned and behind the times because we are reluctant to go down the road. The world accepted homosexuality decades ago; the church is now just beginning to accept it. That is the kind of lag that there is. Christians just slowly follow the world downhill. Divorce is becoming as frequent within the church as it was outside it.

These are not horror stories, I am just setting a scene. There is now a new Bible—officially produced by major denominations in America, called the "Inclusivist" version in which all "sexism" has been removed. Jesus is no longer "Son of Man", he is "Child of human being". God is no longer "Father", he is "Father-Mother". The whole Bible has been retranslated and altered quite deliberately, and it is officially the Bible of whole major denominations. It has not yet got over here but it is coming. A reviewer of that version – and I thought it was one of the wittiest and cleverest remarks I had heard – said: "The devil must be laughing her head off." That is not just a joke because in the Inclusivist version the devil is still male, which rather gives the game away, doesn't it?

A BBC morning service took to praying to "Mother" in heaven. I wrote a letter to them and I got the reply from the BBC: "We've had very few objections and we have to reflect current trends in our religious services."

I could take you to an Anglican cathedral where they have installed a new crucifix above the high altar. It is life-size, and on it the figure purporting to be an image of Christ is totally nude. The humiliation of crucifixion included nudity, but the church of the Middle Ages did not want people to know Jesus was circumcised and a Jew. That is another story. On this particular crucifix the crucified figure is depicted as female. Men have told me that they have often had trouble with wrong thoughts when they come to communion. It seems as though the devil tries to rob you of the holiness of communion by putting wrong thoughts in your mind. Can you imagine leaning down in front of a naked female figure when you take the bread and wine? Well, this is happening and if you don't realise it then open your eyes. The utter confusion between male and female has spread right into the church now, and we have it to face inside. The whole question of the ordination of women was simply the tip of the iceberg. I predicted then that the next decision would be the ordination of homosexuals, and I am not going to tell you what I predict will follow that. It is all part of a move in which the church is accepting the spirit of the age rather than asking the Holy Spirit to be their leader.

I think you have got the burden. Our society needs strong families and a strong church, and both need strong men. A bishop has written a little poem which I will quote in conclusion: "Where the warfare is fiercest, in the battlefields of life, there you will find the Christian soldier, represented by his wife." He has got something. In the next chapter I want to talk about the differences between male and female which God made and intended. I have discovered that men do not know the difference between men and women. Isn't that astonishing?

2

MALE AND FEMALE

We know it says in the beginning of the Bible that God made us male and female. He made us different. We are of equal value in his sight, equal dignity before him, equal status, but we are different and it is those differences that we need to understand, not only if we are to fulfil our own role and responsibility but if we are to appreciate the other gender. To appreciate women: what they can do that men can't; as well as what men can do and they can't. God made us complementary, not just within marriage but within society generally. We have different contributions to make which are both needed, and we need each other. I want to start with the physical difference between men and women. Did you know what that is? You know a bit of it. When did you first find out?

We all found out these differences either behind the bike shed at school or in all kinds of funny ways – not always from our parents, but we notice the difference, and the most obvious of course is the difference between our reproductive organs. That very difference points to a basic and fundamental difference in the whole of our personality. It is quite clear from the way we are made physically that the male is to take the initiative. It is he who penetrates the female and her body is built to respond to his initiative. He takes the first step and she responds to that – her body does that, but not just her body, her mind and her spirit will respond to the male initiative. She is built that way.

Even within the womb, after intercourse, it is the male sperm that is taking the initiative, swimming up to find that female egg. The male is in a sense active in that conception and the female is passive – not totally passive, for as soon as the sperm enters the egg there is immediate response, but all that reproductive system with which we are only too familiar tells us that the male is responsible and the female is responsive. That is the heart of the basic difference between them.

That is why I wrote the book *Leadership is Male*. It was probably the best known and least read book of 1988. I really got attacked for writing that book. I have had hundreds of letters of thanks for it, and every single one was from a woman. I discovered that most women are longing for men to take the lead. They want their man to be strong. They want their man to be responsible and make decisions — most of them.

There are a few very strong feminists who disagree with that, but when I make that statement in a women's setting, the response is very positive. The first time I spoke on this subject was in Dusseldorf, Germany at the European convention of Women's Aglow. I was the only man in a hall of hundreds of women and I said this and the response was overwhelming. Many of them told me afterwards: we want men to be like this, we want them to lead; our problem is they won't. So the man is to be responsible and the woman responsive.

Let me say something else now: many marriages have been ruined on the honeymoon precisely because young men have not been told this difference. To put it very simply, a man can reach climax in intercourse very quickly indeed – a minute, two minutes; the average woman takes twenty to twenty-five minutes to respond to the point where she climaxes and experiences the pleasure. So many men are ruining their marriages by not being responsible enough to restrain themselves until their wives can join them in what God designed to be one of the most exquisite pleasures on earth.

You can see what I am saying: even in intercourse the man needs to exercise responsibility. Otherwise his wife is not going to get pleasure and it won't be long before he comes home and finds a little note on the kitchen table: "Your slippers are in the fridge and your supper is in the dog and I've gone to bed with a headache." That kind of reaction is saying: "I'm not putting up with it. It is no pleasure to me" – and God intended it to be. But it won't be if the man doesn't exercise responsibility for his wife in that. I will tell you this: couples that have learned that, to share that pleasure together at the same moment, have found one of the greatest secrets of staying together. Everybody is aware of those differences I hope, but there are many other physical differences which we are not aware of until it is pointed out.

For example our bone structure: our skeleton is quite different. That is why a forensic scientist, after a skeleton has been dug up that has been buried for twenty years or much, much longer – even an Egyptian mummy – can say with confidence whether it is a woman or a man, because the bones are different. The man's bones are thicker and stronger and altogether rougher than the delicate bones of a woman. Our muscles are quite different. A man's muscles are primarily designed for pushing and pulling – that kind of movement. "Striates" is the technical term for a man's muscles. A woman's muscles are primarily built for carrying, particularly in the pelvic region, but throughout her body. I have been amazed when I have gone to African nations or other countries to see the loads that women can carry on their heads while keeping their backs straight. They can carry immense loads. My wife can lift far heavier things than I can credit her. But for pushing and pulling, no – therefore, if you are having to kick start the car by pushing it, then you push it and get your wife to steer. But you should tell her what to do. You are much better at pushing and pulling, and she is better at carrying. I read of a Scotsman in the Hebrides who landed himself in the hospital with a double rupture. When the doctor asked him what he had been doing to get this he said, "I was lifting a heavy crate onto my wife's back." There is a truth in that actually. Our bones are different, our muscles are different, our fat is different. It is disposed in a different way. We all know where it comes to in a man. I was talking to a man with a huge beer belly and he said, "It's all right, the fat belongs to the Lord and it's all paid for" – but that's where it comes for us. You know you are in middle age when your age shows around the middle. More than that, our skin is different and this is a very important practical point. In women's skin the nerve endings are much nearer the surface than with us. Our skin is tougher, less sensitive, hers is much more sensitive. A surprising fact, however, is that my wife can lift much hotter plates than I can, which seems to go against that, but nevertheless it is true her skin is far more sensitive than mine and the very practical implication for that is this: a man can get a sexual message only from the skin of certain parts of his body, not all over. A woman can get a sexual message from any part of her skin. Touch does far more to a woman than a man.

The practical implication to that is: first, your wife needs to be touched. One of the ways you can prove that you love her is to touch her, and she gets the message. Many men don't do that, they keep their hands right off their wives and they don't get the message. I want you to imagine a husband and wife and the wife is saying, "Do you still love me?"

"Of course I do." This is the romantic conversation, you understand.

"But you never say so."

"Shouldn't need to, after all these years – I have stayed with you, haven't I?"

This is how to develop a wife's arousal and get her to respond. One touch, one hug would have made that conversation unnecessary. However, in saying that your wife needs to be touched, it means being careful about touching other women. We have now entered a new phase of church life where there is a lot of "huggy kissy" fellowship around and we need to learn the difference between a kiss and a holy kiss. Do you know the difference? Two minutes. Sometimes I stand around at the church door and watch the pastor, and I have noticed some pastors give hugs and lovely kisses to all the young, pretty wives but the dear old age pensioners who have lost their looks get a good handshake. Touching is important; skin is much more sensitive in a woman.

Our mortality is very different. We men are weak – the weaker sex at both ends of life. As babies we are the weaker; as old men, we are the weaker. That is why there are more widows than widowers by far. At the time of birth the death rate ratio is 106 males to 100 females. So even at birth we are still the more prone to perish. The ratio does not equalise until the age of four. At the other end of life, it swings right back the other way and even further, and my average life expectancy is a good deal less than my wife's, as any insurance company will tell you. We are weaker at both ends of life but stronger in the middle. That is a difference that is biological.

Let us consider breasts for a moment. What is their significance beyond the obvious one of feeding of a baby? For this we have to turn to the Song of Solomon in the Bible, where in Chapter 1 the young lady says about a young man: "My lover is nestling between my two breasts." Not my baby is, my lover is.

There it is in the Word of God, and I read one commentary on that book which said the two breasts symbolised the Old and New Testaments. I thought, "Help!" Well that puts the man in the Apocrypha for a start, but I really developed a guilt complex, I thought, "I must be a very carnal old man because when I read that verse I don't think about the Old and the New Testaments." I thought, "Should I confess this? I was thrilled when I discovered the Song of Solomon was not written in code, it is not an allegory, it is a simple analogy of a love between a young man and a young woman – and it is an analogy of the love we can have with the Lord. When the Lord says two breasts, he means two breasts. When he says pomegranates he means pomegranates. The Lord means what he says. I was released, and there in the centre of the Bible is this erotic love song. It has got nothing about God, nothing about heaven, nothing about salvation – there is nothing "spiritual" in it at all. It is all about the love between a young man and a young woman. It is God's way of saying, "I made that. I intended that." Therefore, in the human species breasts are for the comfort of adults as well as the nourishment of babies – they are for comfort and companionship with someone of the other sex within marriage.

Blood is different, hormones are different, the nervous system is different, brains are different. I am not going into all these differences now but I wanted to pick up the brain thing and move on to the psychological differences, which are even more important for men to realise, especially within a close relationship of marriage. If you do not realise the differences of thinking and feeling then you are liable to judge your wife by yourself, and misunderstand quite deeply, and this becomes frustrating to a wife. Now let us look at these psychological differences.

Our brain is in two hemispheres. There are two parts to it. I am sure you will have seen pictures of the brain, clearly in two lobes, and men use one side primarily and women use the other. There is a move today to persuade us each to use the other side more. For example, art classes drawing with the other side of the brain is a course my wife once took. It was fascinating that she had to struggle to use the other side of her brain to draw the side that a man would normally use for perspective and three dimensions, but which she would not. A man on the whole trusts his intellect much more than a woman, where she will trust her intuition. Again, they are different sides of the brain.

Let us take one of the more obvious differences: language is on the women's side of the brain. Linguistics are much easier for a woman than a man. Or, to put it very simply, a man will find it far more difficult to put his thoughts and feelings into words than his wife will. A wife can immediately talk about her innermost tensions, feelings, thoughts—pour it out. A man is almost tongue-tied when asked about, "What's your greatest fear? What's your greatest temptation?" He will not know how to put it. This has a profound effect that she finds it easier to communicate with him than he does with her. Probably the breakdown of communication is responsible for more breakups in marriage than almost anything else. It affects church life too. When you have an open time of prayer in your church, who prays first: a man or a woman? Who prays most, the men or the women? You check it out next time. Many Christian couples know that they should be praying together but they don't. The reason is that they tried and came unstuck because she just poured out her heart, prayer after prayer, and kept going, and he, after a few sentences, gets stuck and does not know what to say next. We have to learn to pray aloud. It does not come naturally. This is why most translators and interpreters in places like Brussels and the United Nations are women. They can handle two languages at once—this is their gifting.

It is their side of the brain. Men can develop speech but it does not always come naturally.

Have you ever noticed how often, when a couple is interviewed on television after some domestic disaster, the husband sits there in silence while his wife does all the talking to the camera? Do you know that is as old as the garden of Eden? I don't know if you realise that when Satan spoke to Eve, Adam was standing right there. Satan never addressed him and Adam never addressed Satan. He left his wife to do all the talking, and that is where it all went wrong because she misquoted the Word of God which had been spoken to Adam. She got it wrong and he should have corrected her immediately and said that God didn't say that. For example, Satan said to Eve, "Has God told you not to eat any of the fruit of the trees of the garden?" That was not what God had said, and Adam should have come in straight away and said, "You're wrong," but Adam just stood there saying nothing, and he allowed Eve to be deceived – taken into a conversation she couldn't handle, into a situation she couldn't resist. He said and did nothing which is why, in the rest of the Bible, Eve is not blamed for the first sin on earth. Adam is held responsible and he was responsible.

This is a thing we have got to battle with – it is why in a men's discipling group we need to learn to pray aloud, to speak our thoughts, to get it out, to share with one another how we feel, what we are struggling with. It is a big barrier and it will only be overcome within an all-male brotherhood. I have learned that you cannot disciple men in a mixed group. Men will never open up about their innermost fears, problems, doubts, in front of their wives and children. They want their family to see a strong image of a man who can handle life, and that is right, but that man needs a brotherhood where he can speak it out and share—it doesn't come naturally.

Of course, when a man is baptised in the Holy Spirit and filled with the Holy Spirit, one of the first things that happens is he is released in speech, and most of the gifts of the Spirit are speech gifts: word of wisdom, word of knowledge, word of prophecy, word of tongues, word of interpretation. Most of the gifts that God uses to do good in this world are speech gifts. Indeed, he brought the whole universe into being with a word. But if we men suffer from lockjaw and the church is full of silent male saints, then the world is going to suffer and even the church will be at loss. Men need to be released in speech.

It does not come naturally but I can tell you that when I first began to preach in church I was so nervous I drained every glass of water in every pulpit. It was someimes an interesting study in pond life, after which I had diarrhea for days! I did from time to time suffer from nerves, but I have had to learn to use the other side of the brain, and the Spirit has enabled me to do that.

Let us look at some of the other simple differences. A man can think in abstract terms, but many women think in terms of the concrete. The man thinks about the theory, but she is very practical and will say, "How does it work out?" She thinks in pragmatic terms. A man can talk about things endlessly, whilst at the same time his wife will be talking about people. A bunch of men at one end of the room will be talking about motorbikes or football whilst a bunch of women on the other will be talking about the men on the other end of the room. Their interest is in people.

When I went to Australia I thought I was going to a man's country and I made an astonishing discovery. In Australia the men are only men when they are among men. That is in the bar or wherever, the football – they are men among men. But when they get among women they turn into mice. When my wife was with me and we went to a social event, within five minutes all the men were at one end of the room and the women at the other end and they never met again. She could not cope with that at all. Mixed company was a situation where men zipped up their lips and stayed totally silent. Therefore, in the homes and in the churches it was the women who took the lead every time. They spoke out.

I said to a sociologist: "This country is the most matriarchal country I've ever been in, not excluding the United States. The women run the home and the church."

He replied, "Yes, we even have coined a special word for it, for Australian men, 'Matridoxy'."

I asked, "Why, what's behind this?"

He said, "It's the fact that Australia was a penal colony. New Zealand wasn't. New Zealand actually was a Christian settlement, hence the name 'Christchurch', but Australia was a prison. In the early decades there were nineteen men to one woman, and she was probably a prostitute. There was no normal social intercourse and the men didn't have the opportunity to develop normal social relations with women and that shadow is still over them."

On one visit I said: "Please make all the meetings men only. I have a burden for the men of Australia, and when I got off the jumbo jet, the man who had arranged the visit said, "I'm very sorry David but only one meeting in each place is for men."

"But why? I didn't say that was a personal preference but I believe God gave me the burden to come to Australia for the men."

He responded, "Well the women wouldn't wear it." The first place I went to will be nameless. The men's meeting was on the first night – one thousand men, and we had a great time. The next night was mixed, and as soon as it was over, a lady came up to me afterwards and said to me, "Mr Pawson I have some questions about what you said last night."

"But you weren't here last night," I replied.

She said, "No, but I have got some questions about what you said."

"How do you know what I said last night?"

I made her tell me—when her husband got home she pinned him up against the kitchen wall and said, "What did he tell you?" and she had demanded to know everything – to spill the beans before he got his beans on toast. That was it.

We dealt with her and another, large lady came forward with a small man a yard behind her. She said, "My husband has a question about what you said last night."

I thought, "What is happening?" and I said, "Is that your husband behind you?"

"Yes. This is his question."

I literally pushed her out of the way and pulled him forward by the lapel, and I said, "You can ask me yourself. What's your question?"

He said, "Can a woman be an elder in the church?"

I asked him, "Why – is she? Is she an elder at home as well?" His eyeballs rolled like a jackpot machine.

You might laugh at him, but I tell you there are so many marriages like that. You see, that man had married his "mother". I don't mean his physical mother. I mean that when he left home and left his own mother, he looked for a wife who would be his mother, a substitute mother, and in fact had she been talking about her son like that I would not have even thought it out of the way. Would you? If he had been her little boy and she had come and said, "My boy has a question about what you said," would you have thought that was funny? No. It told me that in their marriage she was like his mother. He probably wanted it that way at first, but was now finding that it was not what makes a good marriage. Now it is nice to be mothered when you are sick or tired, but if that is the whole of the relationship, it is not a

Christian marriage. She is your wife, not your mother. That is why one of the hardest things you could say to your wife is: "You don't make Yorkshire pudding like my mother used to." You are making a comparison between her and mother, which is not the right comparison.

We are thinking about the difference between men and women, and learning about our roles and responsibilities. So let us take a few other differences. In music, men compose and women arrange. You will find that men do most of the composing with music, though women have been free for centuries to write music, but it is men who do it. The women are good at arranging music once it has been composed. Or take mathematics: many men find mathematics comparatively easy; many women find it much harder.

Let us take a thing like chess: there are about fifty-four world chess masters and about five hundred champions. You can count the women in both groups on one hand. Chess is a man's game because it requires a lot of thinking through, working out mentally; it is essentially a male game. Let us take a few other instances. Men like to tackle big things; women can care for little things. Does your wife have a list of little jobs waiting to be done? Or is it even a big list of little jobs waiting to be done? Let me have an imaginary conversation: Wife—"The kitchen tap is dripping." Husband—"Well, be patient; you know I'm going to build you a new kitchen. I have chosen the cabinets, I've got it all planned. Give me time and you are going to get a whole new kitchen."

"But I just want the dripping tap sorted out."

That is too little a detail for men. We want something big.

"There are a few weeds in the flower bed that need digging out."

"Look I'm planning a rockery and pond for there and I will have it built in no time. You wait."

You see, we tackle big challenges; the detail is not so easy to come by.

Let me come to some of the much more fundamental differences. The great debate in all this, by the way, is whether this is conditioned or constitutional. Are we born with these differences or are they imposed on us by our upbringing?

The humanist's answer is constantly saying these differences are purely the result of environment and education. It is the way we bring up boys and girls that makes the differences. If we change all that, then we can produce persons who are neutral in these ways and not different. Actually, modern research is heading right back in the opposite direction and saying these differences are born in us. For example, if you set a small boy and girl to draw and say that they can draw anything they like, from the boy expect something mechanical and the girl will usually draw something domestic. At four or five months, a girl can recognise a person in a photograph. A boy will take many more months but he will respond to a mechanical toy immediately at five months.

There are many other differences. If you want to study all these you could buy a fascinating little book which my wife has read, entitled: "Why Men Don't Iron". It is a very clever title but after she read the book my wife said, "I really understand you better now than I ever did." Well, we need to understand wives too, and these differences. They are born with us. It is not education or environment that makes these differences. Education picks up the differences. Let me share with you one of the most serious developments in our society. Not only are our churches being increasingly feminised but our schools are too. Our whole educational system for decades has been gradually changed to a feminine education. Now suddenly we are waking up to the fact that the boys are way behind the girls in academic achievement. You must have noticed the headlines. What led up to this? The answer is this: that boys need competition to motivate them to learn. Boys need to be competitive with someone else, but competition has increasingly been crushed out of education. Exams are increasingly politically incorrect because people pass or fail. Everybody must pass. I am sure you are aware of this whole trend, and the result is that our whole educational system now is heavily weighted in favour of girls. Of course our employment system is also weighted that way, because two-thirds of all the jobs that are available now go to women. Unemployment now is becoming a male problem.

We can consider the fundamental differences and here is one – for a moment forget all the others. A man is goal-orientated but a woman is need-orientated. Let us explore that a bit. A man, to fulfil his potential, must have a goal in front of him that he has not reached. He must have a purpose to go for, even getting up in the morning. He must feel he has something to aim at, something to achieve that day. That is what motivates him. This is why unemployment hits men far worse than women because it robs a man of getting up in the morning with a goal. This is why there is so much midlife crisis among men, because by the age of forty most men have reached their goal. Sportsmen have reached it even earlier.

The problem becomes: what do you go for now? You have climbed the mountain, you found there is little there, so what is the next mountain? That is when many men go a bit crazy in the midlife crisis. It has nothing to do with hormones, it is simply that a man has reached his goal and does not know where to go next, so suddenly he heads off into the blue to sail around the world; he trades in his wife for another model, and starts driving his sports car again – and he is looking for a new goal. Men in their forties often have this crisis because most men have gone as high up on the ladder as they are going to get by that age, and now they are faced with twenty years more stuck at that level. You know this happens, and that men need a goal to go for. They need a future that they have not reached.

What an advantage it is to be a Christian because you will have a goal to reach for until your dying breath. Many men who retire are dead two or three years later because they no longer have a goal. They no longer have a purpose. We must have a goal, something to aim for, however small or however remote. We are goal-orientated and this means that men live for the future. We live for something on ahead, not the now – we live for the "then" and we have got to have something in the "then" that keeps us going to reach it and we set ourselves all kinds of goals – political, commercial, financial status, but we go for it and that is what keeps men going. Women don't need that at all, and we should not expect them to.

Women are need orientated and they are most fulfilled when they are meeting an immediate need. Even just saying in a crisis "I'll put the kettle on" does something for a woman. It helps her to cope with the crisis. A man will stand there and think of the consequences of all this, and "What is this all going to mean?" whereas she says "What can I do now to meet this need?" Unemployed women can usually find needs that they can still meet, even on a voluntary basis, without being paid. Men without the goal are lost. They feel they are of no value, that society does not value them. Whether they are paid adequate social security benefit or not is beside the point. They have been robbed of their fundamental reason for existence, but women, being need-orientated, live in the present. They tend not to think ahead too much. They think about the now.

To illustrate this in a humorous way, and this is the only criticism of my wife you will hear. It is when we go into unknown territory in the car and I drive and she navigates. Am I touching a chord? She responds to the immediate situation while I think ahead. Often, if I have time, I get a road atlas out and I trace my journey and all the numbers of the roads, and I know when I should be looking for the A429 and the A2. I think ahead all the time.

My wife sits by my side and says, "We should have turned left at the last crossroads"; or in the middle of the traffic lights: "Quickly turn right" – whatever traffic is all around – crisis! I keep saying to her: look at the map and count the number of roundabouts we have to pass before we reach that one. Or just notice when we have to turn; but no, she sits in the present and she responds to the present all the time. It is just an illustration. I need to understand that for her to plan a road map route is quite an exercise. She has got to use the other side of her brain, and I am beginning to get a little educated in this and she is getting better. I hope I am getting a better driver too.

The other huge difference is that a man can split himself up into parts. A woman will always act as one whole. She does not like a life that is in compartments. She wants the whole of life to be a single integrated experience. That is why a woman who goes out to work will take photographs of her family to show others at the workplace – a thing that a man does not usually do. She wants her workplace and her home to be integrated. She wants her people at work to know about her life and the family. She wants to bring them together. She is constantly unifying her life into one life.

A man on the other hand can live four or five totally different lives simultaneously. He can be one person at work, another in the club, another at home, and never will these different lives meet. He just adapts. I noticed some men who are very shy in the church, but when I go and visit them at work, and especially if they wear a uniform, they are totally different. They are commanding, they are strong, in charge, and yet in another part of their lives they are quite sheepish. We are able to adapt, therefore this is a very practical word for men. Men can be in love with more than one woman, but a woman cannot be in love with more than one man. Now this is a very important difference. It means that we men have temptations that women don't have.

A man can quite easily cope with three different women in his life, and have an entirely different relationship with each one. He can have a wife. He can have a mistress at work. He can visit a prostitute for excitement. He can say, "I'm in love with all these women."

One day his wife finds out and she says "You don't love me any more."

He says, "What makes you say that?"

"Well, I've heard all about the other women that you love so you can't love me any more."

He says, "But I do, I do," and he does with part of himself.

But it is a compartment, it is one kind of love, and he feels he needs another kind of love so he has another woman for that. This was common in the Roman Empire when the New Testament was written. It was normal for a man to have a wife and a concubine and still visit prostitutes. He was having different kinds of love in the different situations, and within the situations he loved them all. That is why most of the words in the Bible about sexual temptation are addressed to men.

On the other hand, a woman can love one man at once and therefore – and here is something very important – if her husband really loves her, and she feels that, she will never look at another man. She may have friends, other men, but she won't love any other man if she is really loved by her husband. So, when a husband tells me his wife has gone off with somebody else, my first question is, "Did you really love her and did she realise that? If she did, she would never have looked at anybody else." A wife is not going to go off with the milkman if she is really loved by her husband – it doesn't happen! But the husband has the problem and I have heard many people, Christians even, justify divorce and remarriage because they say, "But don't you see, I fell in love with somebody else" – as if that justifies breaking up the marriage. It is perfectly possible to fall in love with somebody else, but it does not make it right to say, "I must get out of this marriage and follow that one." This is because we are compartmentalised. That is both our strength and our weakness. Just as a woman's desire to have an integrated life is her strength and her weakness. To put it simply, a man can separate his thoughts from his feelings, but a woman can't. Her thoughts and feelings are totally bound up together, and this is why you can argue with a man but not with a woman. If you argue with a man, it is thoughts challenging thoughts, but it does not necessarily affect the feelings you have for somebody.

Since the House of Commons began to be televised I have been embarrassed by the way they slang each other across the House. Haven't you? It is dreadful. There the green carpet has two red strips, two sword lengths apart, and they must not put a toe over so they don't come to blows, but they slang each other verbally and call each other all sorts of dreadful things, but those same men you will find treating each other to drinks at the House of Commons bar immediately after the debate. Thoughts had been clashing, and they may have even felt angry or frustrated about the thoughts, but their feelings about each other were not into it.

That is why it is easier for men to discuss something and not break a relationship. Mrs Thatcher was not like that. When she disagreed with a man, she took it personally. So will most women because you are not just sharing thoughts, you are touching their integrated personality. You are touching their feelings, and in disagreeing you are offending feelings as well. That is what happened to Mrs Thatcher when finally the last man with whom she came into government rebelled. She was finished two months later. She had lost every man in her team because she took it so personally. Now that is something we do need to understand. It is why we need to be careful about arguing.

There are two ways men can win an argument with their wives. One is to shut up and refuse to talk any more, just let her let off steam. If you don't do that and go moody and silent, the other way is this. It is when physical abuse comes into the marriage, especially when a man feels that verbally she has won the argument because of her linguistic skill. She won it verbally so he might resort to shutting up or hitting out. That is a pattern which is only too familiar to social workers.

Now I have to point out that this difference is both the strength and the weakness of male and female. I have referred to some of the weakness of the female, but her strength is that she is a source of unity. Women are much better at bringing things together than men are. Men can keep them separate but women can integrate life and bring together, they can unite a family. A grandmother within a family can be a profound influence in keeping the family together.

Now let us consider the male strength and weakness in being able to separate thoughts and feelings. That puts us in an advantageous position to deal with things objectively, whereas the woman is going to handle it subjectively. How she *feels* is going to be a major part of her decision. A man can stand back, as it were, and put his feelings to one side and say, "Now let's reason this thing out and let's look at it objectively. Let's see what's right and wrong in this situation." My wife needs me to do that. Whereas I need her intuition to back up my conclusion. Her intuition works a lot more quickly than my intellect.

We were counselling a vicar and his wife once, for two hours, and I felt I was no nearer the problem. As we came away I said to my wife, "What's wrong with that couple?" She said it was obvious. That is a little irritating, isn't it? It offended my intellect because my intellect had not grasped anything. She said, "The vicar loves his church more than his wife."

I commented, "He never said that."

She said, "He was saying that every time he opened his mouth."

We were able to go back and deal with it. I analysed. I think things through. I come to a conclusion, and usually it is a conclusion my wife came to much earlier.

It is good to have her intuition. On the other hand there are times when she has gone to hear a preacher and she has come away and says to me, "He was very interesting and very impressive, but I was uneasy and I don't know why. My spirit wasn't responding to him."

I reply, "Tell me what he said."

When she tells me and I analyse it in the light of scripture I say, "I can tell you now why you were uneasy." Something was not right. She sensed it but she could not explain it. A husband and wife can be of immense value to each other by the husband explaining things and the wife sensing them. The two can really be quite powerful together.

However, and here I come to something very practical, it means that discipline should be in male hands. A woman will find it very difficult to discipline others because her feelings get in the way. I was speaking some time ago in Grays Inn, London where lawyers have their headquarters. It was a fascinating debate in which I was taking part. The question was this: "Was Jesus a liar, a lunatic or the Lord?"

Well I was really ready for that. The President of the British Secular Society took the line that Jesus was a liar. A Professor of Biology in the University of London took the line that he was a lunatic, and I had to argue that he was the Lord. There were about 250 lawyers there, so I tried to make it a bit of a brief. You may be interested at the voting at the end of the debate. It was five percent in favour of liar or lunatic. Fifteen percent abstained, but eighty percent said he must be the Lord, which was fascinating. A story was going around the lawyers, and the story was that a woman was accused of murdering her husband. All the evidence, eyewitnesses, circumstantial evidence, was pointing to her guilt. The jury could not come to a unanimous verdict, so the judge went for a majority verdict and they produced an eleven to one result: guilty of murder. The eleven were men, the one was a woman. She was asked, "Why did you not vote – she was so obviously guilty of murdering her husband?" To which the woman juror replies, "Well, I was so sorry for her because she is a widow."

Now that may sound thoroughly illogical to you but it is a woman's feelings getting into her decision. The joke has a bit of truth in it.

Men must take responsibility for discipline because discipline means setting aside your personal feelings and asking whether punishment is deserved or not. A wife is right to say to a child who has misbehaved: wait until your father gets home. He must come home and take that responsibility of deciding whether that child should be punished or not. This is why it is so difficult for single mothers to bring up children properly. They either veer toward becoming too soft and letting the children have their own way in everything, or to make up for the husband they become too strict and too domineering. Either way, I have noticed most single mothers go to one extreme or the other. They find it very difficult to be objective about punishment.

Now comes the rub for the church: the missing dimension of the church today in England is discipline. It is hardly ever exercised in church, and in churches that are led by women or have a woman vicar it is never exercised, because a woman finds it so difficult to confront a person with what is wrong and punish if necessary. We are told in the New Testament that we are not to judge people outside the church. When will Christians learn that? We are not to judge immorality outside the church – that is not our business – but we are to judge it inside the church. Yet the church has got very good at condemning it outside and overlooking it inside, because that requires male objectivity. That is why I believe the elders in a church ought to be men. Where the eldership is mixed (or even more where the majority are women, as is now the case in the Church of Scotland) then discipline goes out of the window. It is a man's job to discern wrong and deal with it and apply discipline.

Discipline is part of the New Testament church picture. There is no question about that. There are various steps that the church needs to take when a member is misbehaving and bringing the gospel into disrepute. Step number one is to go privately to that person and say: you are doing wrong; you are letting the side down; you are bringing disgrace on the church and offence to the gospel that you shouldn't have – because the world is very quick to spot faults in Christians, believe me. They really are quicker than we are. "He calls himself a Christian and yet if you study his business accounts you will find something rather different." The world is very quick to judge us. It is one of the ways God keeps us on the straight and narrow – he lets the world see when we are not.

The second step is if the person does not listen to private rebuke and repent and put it right, then you take witnesses with you, and out of the mouth of two or three witnesses the person is told. If he still won't listen, the third step is that you tell it to the church – the whole church – and the whole membership must face the person. If still that person takes no notice then you have no option but to put them out of fellowship, to excommunicate.

Jesus told us to do this, but where is it being done in this country? There is a final step, which is the hardest of all, and I have been involved in just one or two situations of this kind where even being put out of fellowship still has no effect on a Christian who is misbehaving. You have one last thing you can do, one last sanction, and that sanction is to deliver them to Satan, which actually means in practice that you are putting them physically in the hands of the devil so that he can do something to their body that will bring them to their senses. It is the last resort of church discipline but it is saying then Satan must have freedom to bring you sickness or even death if that will save you on the day of judgment. You are doing it to save them, to redeem them, to get them back on course. Now all that requires courage and conviction.

It is not easy to confront people; nevertheless it is part of the picture of the church which we have in the New Testament. I have found that women find it very difficult to do that. Their feelings get in the way. Can I bring it down to brass tacks? I have written a book on hell. It was one of the most difficult books that I have had to write but I felt suddenly some years ago that there was a widespread turning away from belief in hell, set off, I am afraid, by a leading evangelical Christian in this country, John Stott, who admitted quite openly in print that he could not accept hell as eternal torment. Suddenly, everyone else said that if he does not believe it, then we don't need to. Even Bible-believing Christians all over this country suddenly did not believe in hell any more. Actually, I suspect they stopped talking about it years earlier, and now they were relieved, but I wrote the book and it is a call back to Bible teaching on the subject. I called attention to the remarkable fact that within our Bible it is only taught by Jesus, not by anyone else – as if there was only one person that God the Father could trust to give us the right view.

I was interviewed on many BBC local radio programmes about this book, and the interview always began with the same question, which got very boring. The question was: "How can a God of love send anybody to hell?"

My response was to ask a question back. I have learned that from Jesus. The best way to deal with a question is to ask one back. The ball goes in the other court, and my question was: "Where on earth did you get the idea that God was a God of love?"

This shattered the interviewer. They would stammer and stutter and say, "Well, doesn't everybody believe that?"

I said, "Come on, where did you get that idea that God was a God of love?"

Finally, they would say: "Didn't Jesus tell us that?"

I said, "Yes he did, and that is why I believe it, but he was the one who also told us about hell in terms of the utmost horror. Now what are you going to do about that? Are you going to say that he was telling the truth when he said God was love and telling a lie when he talked about hell? That is just hit and miss, isn't it? How do you know when he told the truth?"

Usually the interview would end quite quickly, before time, but it is amazing how many people find it difficult to believe in hell. As the church has been increasingly feminised, hell has gone. When have you last heard it preached about? What I am leading up to is that of course my wife knew about this book. I would go into a garden shed and bury myself for two or three weeks to write a book, and while I was there she would feed me with courage and coffee. She said, "David, while I believe everything you are writing, I couldn't write that book."

I said, "Why not?"

She said, "Because just even talk about hell makes me think of relatives, friends that are going there or are already there. It becomes too much, my feelings get too deep." I can understand that, because I had to weep over people, but I had to write the book. You see what will happen in a church that is feminised is that only half of God will be preached. Paul says, "Behold then the goodness and the severity of God." That is the whole picture. But in a feminised church you will hear about his goodness but not about his severity. And broadcast religion is a classic example. Preachers on television and radio know that people can just switch them off if they say something they don't like. You rarely hear the severity of God preached on television and on radio, do you? Broadcast services, songs of praise, it is all about how nice God is, how loving he is, how helpful he is – all of which is true – but if the severity is not preached I will tell you what will vanish: the fear of God will go and there is as much fear of God in the New Testament as in the Old. We will return to that.

So we have a situation where the people of God need the leadership of men. That is what led me to write the book *Leadership is Male*, and as I have mentioned before and say in the preface of that book, I first gave the material to about fifteen hundred women in Dusseldorf, and at the end of that conference one German woman came to me. She wasn't uptight but she was quite severe, and she said, "Well Mr Pawson we have heard the truth from you and we have seen it in your wife." That is probably the nicest thing that anyone has said about her. I make a joke of it of course, and laugh it off, and say "I preach and she practises; that's how we manage together", but I know that I should be practising too. The church needs men to apply discipline in the church, to challenge what is happening.

I hardly go to a single church today without finding adultery in the church accepted and unchallenged. Either in its crudest form of men who have left their wives and are living with someone else, or in its respectable form: they have ditched their wife and married someone else, which Jesus called adultery. I have been in more trouble for saying that publicly in a ten-year period than anything else I have said. It caused a riot at Spring Harvest and they told me I would never be invited back because I challenge Christians who have left their partners because they prefer someone else, and it is happening all over the church – unchallenged, accepted, and churches are even blessing it.

I have written a book on it because again the Lord has given me a huge burden about it, and I am aware that it is the most sensitive and emotive thing to say, because there are always people in your congregation who are profoundly affected, and most preachers seem to be intimidated to the point where they dare not quote what Jesus said about that issue, but there it is. Men are needed who have the courage. Where are the men who will rise up in anger within the church and say that bishop ought not to be a bishop if he does not believe in the virgin birth or the bodily resurrection? But we let it go by.

This is the second area in church life where men are needed – the area of doctrine; what we believe, not just how we behave. Discipline is needed in the area of behaviour, but in the area of doctrine I have mentioned the subject of hell and the severity of God. It takes men to preach that. I have been preaching on hell quite a lot because nobody else seems to be doing so. It is a costly subject to teach. Yet the response I have had is this: letter after letter saying, "This has restored to me the fear of the Lord." I find that people who don't believe in hell don't fear the Lord. It seems to go together.

It is basically an elective, the fact that God is our Judge. I turned to my Bible to write the book *Leadership is Male* and in one Christian bookshop it was sold in plain brown paper bags from under the counter, as if it was pornographic or something! All the negative reaction I have had has been from people who did not read it, who just assumed from the title that I was an old-fashioned chauvinistic pig, but those who read it came to a different view. This does not put women down at all; it puts men face to face with their *responsibility*.

When we look through the Bible it gives men not the "right" but the responsibility to lead. Right from the beginning: Genesis 2 says three things about Adam and Eve. It says that Eve was made after Adam; Eve was made from Adam; and Eve was made for Adam. And every one of those three things is quoted in the New Testament, talking about relationships between Christian men and women. She was made after Adam means that he was the firstborn and therefore responsible for her. Yet when God challenged him about what happened and challenged him first, "Adam what have you been up to?" Adam shifted the blame; he passed the buck. He said, "It was that woman you gave me." He is blaming her and him. It is an incredible statement. It is always somebody else who is responsible for our mistakes.

So it was right from the beginning, when Adam should have led. Satan, I believe, knew what he was doing when he appealed to Eve as the head of the house and he got her to make the decision, and her to take the lead, and her to take the fruit and then give it to her husband – and he just took it. Satan had reversed the order of men and women and he is still trying to do the same. He is doing it in quite incredible ways.

Let me tell you just one way. A man came to me in Australia, greatly troubled. He said, "David, I've been listening to you; I agree with what you are basically saying and I want to be the head of my house. It is not that I want to be dictator, but I want to be leader."

I said, "Why aren't you?"

He said, "My wife won't let me."

"What hold has she got on you? I think I know. Have you given your manhood to another woman outside your marriage?"

"Yes."

I said then: "That's why she's got a hold on you."

He said, "What do you mean?"

"Well, you gave your manhood to someone else; that's put guilt in your conscience."

He said, "You've probably heard the story many times over. I was working late at the office. There was a very attractive secretary. I met her at the coffee machine. We were the only two in the building and you can guess the rest. We got talking and she was much more sympathetic than my wife is to my problems. We got together and finished up on the floor together. It was only once. I have never done it again, but I made the biggest mistake of my life: I told my wife. I confessed it and she has never allowed me to forget it. Whenever I try to make a decision or take the lead, she points at me and says, 'I wasn't the one to break this marriage up; I wasn't the one to be faithless. I was true to you' – and I just crumble."

You see, a guilty conscience robs you of moral courage. You cannot stand up for what is right when you have got something wrong like that in your conscience, and I had to persuade him very strongly that when God forgives, he forgets. It is so important: that God doesn't hold a thing against you, he forgets it, and one day when you face God and you say, "God, now that I face you and I think of that and I am so ashamed and so sorry,"

God will say, "You did what? I don't remember that."

Isn't that amazing? "I don't remember it. Your sins I will remember no more." That is forgiveness.

One night I was preaching in church and when everybody had gone home there was a little old lady sitting in the front pew, weeping her heart out, and I sat by her and put my arm around her and said, "What's the matter?"

She said, "Thirty years ago I did the most terrible thing. If my family knew about it they would never talk to me again. If it were my friends, then I would have no friends. For thirty years I have asked God to forgive me and he never has."

I said, "You poor soul, he doesn't know what you are talking about."

"What do you mean?"

I said, "The first time you asked for forgiveness he forgave you and he forgot about it. He cannot remember it."

She said, "You can't mean that."

I took her through text after text which says that when God forgives, he forgets. "Your problem is that you cannot forget. It is difficult enough to forgive someone else because you cannot forget what they did, but God controls his memory and he can wipe it clean. That is real forgiveness."

When the old lady realised the truth of it, she got up and danced around the whole church. She was leaping for joy, a lady in her late seventies or early eighties, dancing. Now that is the kind of dancing I would like to see in church. It is not the charismatic two-step, it is something much more real, and she was dancing for joy at the release. This man was not, you see, and his wife kept throwing it in his face and as soon as she did he went silent, he could not say anything. He was intimidated by his own guilt. I persuaded him that God didn't hold it against him and that he could go home and say to his wife, "My God has forgotten what I did and you must too." And he did, and it restored his authority in the home, restored the marriage to a proper Christian pattern, but you see one of the things that unfaithfulness in marriage or even fornication before marriage can do is to rob you of your moral authority within a marriage.

Many men need to have that dealt with so that they can be free in their conscience to tell the family what is right and wrong, knowing that the family cannot hold against them what they have done. All of us have done wrong, all of us have sinned, but it needs forgiving and being dealt with so that we are free to lead in home and church. In the Bible – not only in the beginning when Adam was held responsible for what happened in the garden – from then on, leadership was male all the way through. Israel was led by a series of leaders in three categories: first by prophets, from Moses to Samuel; then by kings from Saul to Zedekiah; and then by priests. They were led by prophets, priests, kings – all male.

When Jesus came to build the church he did not choose six men and six women, as many are saying today that he would if he were starting the church today. He didn't, and that was not because he was (as people say) a child of his time – that he had to accommodate himself to the culture of the day. Jesus never did that. He challenged his enemies about that. He said, "Do I fear God or man? Who do I try and please?" They were silent because they knew he would go right against any tradition, any cultural custom that was not in line with the will of God – but he chose twelve men, and as Paul says in 1 Corinthians 11, the pattern is very clear: God is the head of Christ, Christ is the head of man, and man is the head of woman.

The question arises "What ministry is open to women?" My answer is that every ministry is open to women: evangelistic, pastoral, teaching, prophetic. It is not a question of what ministry is open to women, but the sphere in which it is exercised. If it puts that woman in a position of authority over men, I believe it to be wrong. Women are encouraged to teach, for example, by Paul, and yet he said he would not allow them to teach men – because that puts them in authority over them. Now that is my understanding of scripture: that we men are to take the lead in mixed company, in family and in home. We take the lead; not dictate – that is an abuse of leadership.

Leadership is to be the kind that Christ has for the church; it is loving, sacrificial, considerate, sensitive leadership, but it is nevertheless leadership. We don't tell Christ what to do, Christ tells the church what to do. Similarly, a father has that responsibility within the home of leading the family, not of being a little dictator. My wife constantly reminds me to practise what I preach. It is quite uncomfortable because I am always preaching, and she keeps remembering something I said years ago and says, "You are not practising what you preach." The one thing she constantly says to me is: "I am more than happy to have you as my head when you have Christ as yours." What she is saying is: "I want you to be the kind of head he is."

When men want to be the head of the house without acknowledging that they too have a head, Christ – that is when things go wrong, and a man can become brutal, cruel, a bully within his own family, which is certainly not the will of God. So I believe women can be part of apostolic teams. They can bring prophetic messages. Miriam the sister of Moses did. Deborah did. They can be teachers, pastors, every ministry is open to women, but not in a situation where they are taking authority over men. To me that applies to every group in the church whether it is a small one like a house group or a huge one like the whole church itself. I predict now within thirty years there will be a woman Archbishop of Canterbury. I won't be around to eat humble pie but nevertheless it is inevitable in the present trend.

People are finding ways around it. Most of the new charismatic fellowships know in their heart of hearts that the fellowship should be under the eldership of men, so how have they got around it? They don't have elders. They have what is called a "leadership team", made up of husbands and wives. In almost every case that I know of that, they do not have any single women on the leadership. Now to me that is worst discrimination: to say that you can be a leader if you are married but not if you are unmarried. Where is the biblical basis for that? Nowhere. When I am asked "Can a woman be an elder?" my reply is, "Certainly, if they are the husband of one wife because that's the qualification in scripture." That is a facetious reply but it is really hoping to bring a bit of humour into what can be a very tense discussion.

Now that is my conviction. I don't ask people to agree with me. I ask them to think it through carefully for themselves and to check it out in scripture, because if we are Christians at all then the Bible is our guidebook and it is vital that people should not discuss it in the light of culture or contemporary expectancy. I was disappointed when an Archbishop of Canterbury, at the height of the debate about the ordination of women, said that he was voting for it because the church must be credible to contemporary society. I heard that the Methodist church decided that you don't need to be a believer to be a member. You are free to join the church even if you don't believe in Jesus because they believe that in four or five years' time as a member you will. This accommodation to society is a dead end.

The world despises the church, and the church is constantly cutting its cloth to fit society in the hope of getting more real. The world respects (even if it dislikes) Christians who are different. Who has the courage to say "I will live life God's way, not everybody else's"? It does take courage to run against the tide and somebody wrote to me recently to encourage me after a particularly controversial book I had written, and they simply wrote one line, "David, go with the wind even if it's against the tide."

I thought: "I'm going to live by that." Go with the wind of the Spirit, even if it means going against the tide. Or, as David, on his deathbed, said to Solomon, "Solomon, be a man and keep the statutes of God."

3

HARD AT WORK

When did you last hear a sermon about work? The reason why you don't hear them is that most preachers don't go to work. Many years ago, my son said, "I'm going to be a pastor when I grow up."

I said "Why, Richard?"

He replied, "Because you only work Sundays."

It is a very common impression. Actually, at that time I was on a sixteen-hour day, but I didn't "go" to work and he didn't see me go to work. To most ministers, clergy and pastors, it does not dawn on them that one of the greatest needs of the men in their congregation is to hear what God thinks about their daily work, from Monday to Friday.

The church has left us with a mistaken impression that God is far more interested in what you are doing in church than what you do in the office, the factory, the shop or wherever, which is totally mistaken. We spend about sixty per cent of our waking life at work. Two-thirds of our waking life – and that is all going to be wasted as far as the kingdom of God in concerned unless you understand what God thinks of it. We spend probably thirty to thirty-five per cent of our waking life on family concerns, personal interests, hobbies and sports, and probably five to ten per cent at most engaged in church activities if you are a keen Christian. That means, according to most people's idea, that God is only really interested in five to ten per cent of your life, which is absolutely wrong.

The church has a graded list of jobs in terms of value to God or acceptability to God. "Missionary" is at the very top of the ladder. You become a missionary and you are the best Christian of all. We will even put your photo in the church porch and get people praying for you. Then "evangelist" comes a little bit after that but still quite high, especially if you are someone like Billy Graham. Pastors and clergy come a little lower. Then doctors and nurses are quite valuable to the Lord. They are really serving people's needs. Teachers come usually a bit lower than that. So you come down to taxi drivers and computer operators and their work is as far from the kingdom of God as you can get. Do you see what I mean?

I am not approving this list but often, without realising it, the church is giving that impression. We take far more notice if you are a missionary in Africa than if you are a factory worker in Dagenham. The fault with that lies in this: that factory worker in Dagenham may be more in the frontline of the kingdom of God than the missionary in Africa. Don't misunderstand what I am saying. I have visited missionaries overseas for whom the church is constantly praying, who live in a Christian village with a Christian hospital and a Christian school and nearly everybody in the village goes to church. That lone factory worker in Dagenham is the only Christian on the shop floor. Who needs more prayer?

God would rather have a good taxi driver than a bad missionary. It is not what job you do that God is interested in; it is how you do the job you have. That is far more his concern. I am afraid we don't convey that to our congregations. I advocated a church putting up a photograph of every member of the church to be prayed for, with the mission field in which they operated printed underneath. To take one example, I baptised a young man called Harry Webb. You probably know him as Sir Cliff Richard. We gave him a prayer group to support him in his mission field which was the media world – showbiz. That is one of the toughest worlds in which to be a Christian and he came under terrible attack. We chose people who did not like his music, so they saw him as a brother.

Sad to say, the worst of the attacks that he came under were from Christians. I knew, for example, that at peak viewing time he was actually changing family shows, going through the script with a blue pencil and cutting out whatever he could not accept as a Christian. He was virtually censoring a top family show and keeping it healthy for children. Yet he got letters from Christians: "What are you doing on such a worldly show?" So he needed support; he was right in the frontline.

Now, every Christian is in the front line, whatever job they have. The only jobs that are not Christian are immoral or illegal occupations. Everything else is sacred to God and I cannot stand Christians telling me "I'm in a secular job." I correct them immediately.

I was sitting next to a young man in church and I said, "What are you doing now?" He said, "I'm back in a secular job."

I said, "What do you mean?"

"Well, you know I was a missionary overseas? I've come home and I've got a job in engineering."

I asked, "Why did you call that secular?"

He said, "It is, isn't it?"

I said, "There's nothing secular except sin." You are in a sacred vocation and if you are a better engineer than you were a missionary then God is more pleased with you. He didn't really believe it; I could see it in his face. He felt ashamed and embarrassed to tell me he had stopped being a missionary. Well, let's look at it.

There are two basic wrong attitudes to work: one is to think too little of it and the other is to think too much of it. Those who think too little of work are guilty of what I call the "immorality of the marketplace". What do I mean by that? By the immorality of the workplace I don't mean lewd pin-up pictures about the workbench. I mean something much deeper than that. The immorality of the workplace is to go to work saying, "I will do as little work as possible for as much money as possible, and that is all there is to it." That is an attitude: I'm going to work to "get", not to give, and I will "give" as little as possible and "get" as much as possible. The annual round of demands is simply: less work, more pay; shorter hours, higher wages – constant pressure for those two things.

Now that is immoral. "Oh, it's just a job – a necessary evil which I have to do in order to get money to live." To "live" means weekends primarily, or possibly weeknights. In other words, my real life begins when I get home from work.

I find in conversation at the workplace that the weekend figures prominently: "What are you going to do at the weekend?" Then on Monday: "What did you do at the weekend?" They live for the weekend. There is more calling in sick on Mondays and Fridays than Tuesdays, Wednesdays and Thursdays put together. Why is that? Well, it extends the weekend. Monday or Friday, the two highest reporting sick days, either give you an extra day before you begin the weekend or you have so spent the weekend that, far from it being recreation, it has left you unfit to go to work on Monday morning.

If you are going to work to get as much as you can and to give as little as possible in return, then it won't be long before that immoral attitude makes you do immoral things. For example, it leads to pilfering. The Bible calls it stealing; it can be called "perks". This is especially the case if you work for a big outfit that is not going to miss anything, and especially if there is something lying around doing nothing that you could use at home. "Well, why not take it? Nobody's using it here, nobody's going to miss it, and I'm putting an extension on the house at home and I could do with that...." That is the attitude of someone who went there to get and not to give.

Actually, the big stores lose more from the staff stealing things than from shoplifters. You ask any of them. You will find their bigger bill is staff helping themselves to things and going home with them. Shoplifting is a big issue, especially in Oxford Street stores, but around the country it is staff who feel they have a right to take something home – that it is part of the job.

It is not long before you move on from there to fiddling your VAT returns or your income tax returns to help the business with its cashflow or whatever. So this attitude of "I go to work to get, not to give anything, but to get as much as possible and to give as little as possible" leads on to other things which are clearly wrong. That is what I call the "immorality of the workplace". We used to call it "skiving" in the Royal Air Force. That means to appear to be somewhere where you are not, or to appear to be working when you are not. You work hardest when somebody else's eyes are on you. It is cheating.

The opposite is what I call the "idolatry of the workplace". That makes work your god. You live for your work. Your career takes precedence over everything else, family included: "I am being promoted, we've all got to move, my job is more important than anything else." A Christian family came to me recently and they said, "Will you please pray for our daughter, she's got anorexia and we're very concerned about her — she's going to die." Well, I said, "First let me ask you about yourselves – have you recently moved house?" "Yes, we used to live in the north and we moved south about a year or eighteen months ago."

I said, "Why did you move?" The husband said, "I got a promotion, I got the opportunity – a better job."

I said, "Did you talk that over with your family?"

"Well, no, you get the promotion and you have to go for it."

"You never talked it over with your daughter?"

"No."

"How old is she?"

I think she was about sixteen or seventeen. The whole thing boiled down to the fact that without talking it over, without having been given the reasons for it, she was suddenly uprooted from all her relationships – all of them just went with no consideration. In fact, it was clearly this that lay at the root of the anorexia.

I said to the husband, "How did the new job work out?"

He said, "It didn't, I'm unemployed now." I said, "What a pity you ever left. Did you ask God about it?"

"No," he said. "In our job you just assume that if you don't take promotion, you are finished. If you don't go along with what the boss says." What a cost!

There was a man in America who lived in a wheelchair because he had got polio and would not accept sympathy for his condition. If you tried to sympathise with him he would say, "Thank God for polio."

If you were to ask him, "How can you thank God when you can't move?" He would tell you: "I never slept in a bed; I slept in a train or a plane, so that I could begin business the very next morning. I just kept on the move, from morning till night. Business, business, business. My family was estranged from me. Then I was hit with polio. I've got to know my wife and my kids. We are a happy family. If that hadn't happened to me, the whole family would have been lost." Well, it is a point of view. That was a man who had made his job everything.

Even God himself didn't work seven days a week. God

could take time away from his work and we certainly need to. If your work has become everything, then it is your religion, it is your "god". You are devoting your whole life to it. That is the idolatry of the workplace. Whether it is the success, the status or the power or the sense of achievement or the wealth or whatever makes you do it, you have made your work your god if it comes before everything else in your life. Religion and work have got separated in both cases. Whether you go for the immorality that takes far too low a view of work, or the idolatry that takes too high a view, religion and work get separated. You may go to church on Sunday, but your faith is really not relating to what you do between Monday and Friday at all. There are many for whom Christianity is a spare-time hobby, a personal interest to be followed outside of work. Again, what a waste of all that time. Let me just remind you of a saying that was very popular in the past but which is still relevant: "If he's not Lord of all, he's not Lord at all." That is true when you think it through. Clearly there is somewhere between these two extremes—a right attitude to work, a biblical attitude to work, and that is what we are going to think about now.

One of the reasons why we have got into wrong thinking is that the church has been far too heavily influenced by Greek thinking rather than Hebrew thinking. I have written a short book about this entitled *De-Greecing the Church*. Of course, Western culture is Greek through and through. Until the invention of reinforced concrete and steel, our public buildings were like Greek temples. Town halls looked like the Parthenon; Leeds library, straight from Athens – Corinthian columns; consider St Paul's Cathedral and the Royal Exchange in London. You walk around the city and you will find Greek architecture staring you in the face. Where did the British get their love of sport from? Football is the religion of the majority of the men in this country. They don't mind aerobic worship in the stadiums. Goal – throw the hands up! Ask them to do that for the Lord on a Sunday morning and you are really asking something! Where did we get our love of sport from? Not from the Bible. The Bible has almost nothing about sport in it. About the only text I can think of is: bodily exercise profits little. How about saying that in the modern world? People ask me what exercise I take. Preaching is the main one! We have such sedentary occupations these days that many of us need a bit of exercise. Driving is not a substitute for exercise! However, the Bible doesn't talk about sport, except the illustration of running the Christian race, but sport does not figure in the Bible; it is not in Hebrew thinking. We got it from Greece; we got it from Olympus and the Ionic games. Where did we get our political thinking from? We didn't get it from the Bible. There is not a thing in the Bible about democracy.

I remember going to see the film *The Ten Commandments*. Cecil B. DeMille came onto the screen at the beginning and said, "I wanted to show you the beginnings of Western democracy." There is not a bit of democracy in the Bible, not a shred of it. It is all kingdoms with the king ruling and making the laws himself. Where did we get democracy from? Greece. I could go on but our whole educational system is Greek in its essential thinking and this has profoundly affected the church and us.

The Greeks basically got this wrong. They separated the physical and the spiritual. They never could get them together. They divided life into sacred and secular; your spiritual activities and your other activities. They divided heaven from earth; they put God outside time and made him timeless, which the Bible doesn't. So they divided life up and therefore they divided us into thinking sacred and secular and we have been doing it ever since. The physical world became unspiritual.

I will bring this right down to earth. There is a prayer in the Jewish book of prayers to pray when you go to the toilet. Isn't that delightful? You thank the Lord your body is working properly. You thank the Lord that you feel relieved and you feel better and you come out praising. When I say that to a Jewish audience, and I often speak to Jews, nobody smiles. They just say, "But, of course!" Since I stay in many Christian homes as I travel, I use a lot of Christian loos. There is often a pile of devotional books at the side of the throne. There are texts framed on the walls – all to get my mind off what I am doing in there. God made your body and he is interested in your body— as interested as you. In fact, when you get a bit older and if you begin to lose control of your bowels and bladder, you will wish you had praised the Lord whenever it was working properly. We often finish up in nappies, we men at the end of life. My father did. It is humiliating going back to being a baby.

You see, God is interested in all that. He made the physical world. He is not just going to save your soul; he is determined to save your body too. That is the gospel; that is Hebrew thinking. Life as a whole, physical and spiritual, belong together. There was a man called Augustine who began to split them and replace Hebrew thinking in the church with Greek thinking, and that led directly to the celibate priesthood, in which you were holier if you didn't have sex. He said even sex within marriage is concupiscence. Ever since then we have kept the physical and the spiritual so far apart that somebody who is doing manual labour thinks God has no interest in that whatsoever. Do you see what I mean? The church has picked that up.

So, for the church discipleship has become what I do in my spare time. There are so many discipleship courses going around, from the Alpha to everything else. Not one of them talks about your daily work. They all tell you how to be a

Christian in your spare time; how to read your Bible, how to pray, how to witness, how to do this, that and the other. If they encourage you to witness at work they are encouraging you to steal time from the boss. God did not send you to your job primarily to witness to people. If you do that, be sure to do it in your own time and not in the boss's because that is stealing, but do you see what I mean?

So Christianity has become a leisure pursuit, and again the Greeks lived for leisure, not for work. They tried if they could to get thirty pieces of silver, which was the going price for a slave, so they could buy a slave and not work any more, and get the slave to do their work for them. Two-thirds of the people in Greece were slaves – usually foreigners brought in to do the dirty manual labour, which, frankly, is happening in Europe today. We import immigrants to do the manual work for us. That is what Greece did, only they did it by buying them as slaves. The Greek man lived to become a gentleman of leisure. He loved being able to afford not to work so that he could devote himself to his own chosen pursuits rather than having to do what other people told him to do.

This developed in ancient Greece a whole leisure industry. They had discussions on a place called Mars Hill in Athens, where Paul preached. They had plays – tragedies and comedies. They had their own leisure industry, and, of course, that is where sport developed. You have got to fill your leisure time with something. So, they built their leisure centres. Does all this sound vaguely familiar? People have time on their hands and they have to fill it with something.

Of course, another way to get out of work is to win the lottery – to get the big money as soon as possible so you need not work again. The best cure for wanting that is to read what has happened to the people who won it. Some were wise enough to stay at work, but very few. Most said: "Now I'm free not to work, and to do what I want to do." That is essentially what leisure offers: the choice to do what you want to do rather than what the boss wants you to do. So we have become a weekend society. We live for one weekend and then the next. We live for leisure. We find most purpose in life in leisure. The Hebrews did not have leisure, they worked six days and they worshipped one day.

Some years ago there was a big Christian crusade called "Keep Sundays Special" to try to keep shops and garages shut on Sundays. I wrote an article for a national magazine at that time which drew an awful lot of fire. I called it "Keep Mondays Special". What I said then was as follows:

I hear so many Christians say we must keep Sundays free from work; I haven't heard one of them appealing to the fourth commandment to say we must return to a six-day working week. They were only taking half the law of God. One bit of the law says remember the Sabbath day to keep it holy. "Six days shall thou labour" – no one wants to read that bit nowadays. We even want a four-day week if we can get it. I am being a bit sarcastic but I am trying to paint a picture. No longer do we feel that God is interested in our work or that our work is where we must find our main expression of purpose in life as God intended. Our Christianity has become a leisure pursuit to the point where a Christian man who cannot get to the church prayer meeting because he has had to work overtime is pitied, not prayed for. He somehow let the society down and he develops a guilt complex and says to the pastor on Sunday, "I'm sorry I couldn't get to the church prayer meeting, I had to work overtime." That prayer meeting should have been praying for him in his own time because he was serving God. That is the last thing they think of doing. They noticed his absence.

Now let us go to the Bible. Let us look at three things: creation, the Fall, and redemption. Let us look at what work was originally in God's creation. It will come as a shock to you that Adam had a seven-day working week. He had no Sunday, no Sabbath. He worked seven days a week. Contrary to some Christians' ideas, the Sabbath, the seventh day rest, did not appear until the time of Moses. That, of course, is when Genesis 1 appeared as well. Adam did not know that God worked six days on creation, then rested on the seventh. Because we read it in Genesis 1, we wrongly assume that he knew about it. He did not, and he was never told to keep one day in seven different. The only commandment he was given was "Don't touch that tree in the middle of the garden," but he was told nothing about resting from his work.

His work was comparatively easy. He was looking after an orchard. To get food he had to pick fruit. Adam was not put on earth to worship God all the time. He was put on earth to look after the garden, to work with his hands. Incidentally, working with your hands is the highest form of work in God's sight, even if it is the lowest form of work in your neighbours' sight. Manual labour has the highest dignity in my Bible. I will come back to that. So God put Adam to work and intended him to find fulfilment in that – to enjoy it, to find the purpose in his life, the role of gardener. Yes, he met the Lord at the end of the day to talk things over, how the day had been; he heard the sound of the Lord walking in the garden at the end of the day, but he was there for work.

What is your idea of heaven? I mean spiritually. I will tell you what I find most Christians think it is going to be like: an everlasting Sunday morning service where you sing every chorus seventeen million times. That is the idea that most people have picked up from the church. They get the idea that what you do on Sunday morning is what you are going to be doing forever and ever and ever. Well, God's plan for

Adam was not that. It was to work with his hands. That is because God is a worker. The whole universe around us is the result of the work of his hands. The most amazing part of your body is actually your hands and what they can do. God gave us hands, not just to worship with but to work with. They would not have needed separate fingers just to worship with – to be used for work they do.

That is why the Psalmist prays "Establish the work of my hands." He offers his handiwork to the Lord. So, God is a worker, though he does take a day off from creation for himself. The universe is the work of his hands, and when Jesus came to be the Saviour of the world, had you been planning his life you would never have done what his Heavenly Father did and made him a carpenter for eighteen years. Would you have thought of doing that if you had been God and sending your Son to save the whole world? Stick him in a carpentry shop at a woodworker's bench? For eighteen years he was a woodworker and then for three years he was a wonder-worker. If my maths is still correct, eighteen to three is six to one.

Jesus was almost imitating his Heavenly Father. He worked with His hands and that is all he did for eighteen years: chairs, tables, doors, window frames. The Son of God, the Saviour of the world, did that for eighteen years! It was all part of God's plan to save the world. He said, "My Father has worked until now, now I will work." He did take time off for rest, especially for the sake of the disciples, who were worn out by his work and the crowds that came. This tells us three things about work. One: it has dignity. It is not an embarrassing thing to do. Manual labour particularly has dignity. All the great saints in the Bible were manual labourers. They worked with their hands. Moses was a shepherd, David was a shepherd, the apostles were fishermen. Paul was a tentmaker. Manual labour has a special place in God's sight, whether it is skilled or semi-skilled. What a message that is! The church has lost the working man, we are told. Maybe it is because we have never told them that their work is valued by God. They have never seen it that way: manual labour, working with your hands. In fact, the New Testament says that all Christian men should work with their hands. If your daily job is a desk job, a "head" job, then you need in your spare time to work with your hands. There is something about working with your hands that is very therapeutic. It is very rare that a man who does all his work with his hands needs a psychiatrist. I love to watch country programmes on television, partly because of my farming past. A thatcher or a man who has ploughed fields for seventy years – you know the kind of man – is contented, he is integrated, he is happy; he likes his job and he is proud of it when he has finished.

When you have done something with your hands, isn't it satisfying to stand back and look at it? You can see where you have been and your wife telling you what a wonderful job you have done gives you even more pleasure – "What a wonderful husband I have – I never thought you could do that." Working with our hands is tiring but not exhausting. I meet far too many people today who are so stressed by their work that they come home exhausted – not healthily tired but the kind of exhaustion that prevents them from relaxing and even sleeping. That is not God's intention.

There is the dignity of work. Luther said: "All work ranks the same with God." The second thing is that work is a duty – not something to get out of but something that God gave you to do. In fact, the Bible says: "If any man will not work, neither shall he eat." He has no right to food if he refuses to work. It does not say if any man *cannot* work because he is mentally or physically disabled or because there is simply not a job available. It is not about those men but rather those who *will not* work.

Many years ago, a young man came to see me late morning and he sat down in our living room. It came to half past twelve. In the dining part of the room, the table was set for lunch. I noticed that this young man, who was a student, kept looking at the table pointedly. I kept talking to him and finally, in desperation, he said, "When are you going to have lunch?" – clearly inviting himself to share it.

I said, "Well, we're going to have lunch just as soon as you've gone." He looked at me and said, "I was rather hoping to join you."

I replied, "I'm sorry, the Bible forbids me to give you lunch."

"What!"

I took him to that verse, and then I said, "You are a professional student."

Do you know who that is? It is somebody who finishes one course and applies for another, finishes that and applies for another, who just likes studying at the taxpayers' expense and has no intention of ever taking a job; just spending his life taking one course after another. You can get away with it if you are reasonably convincing, and he got away with it for nine years and had no intention whatever of ever repaying society for all that had been invested in him. I knew that.

He professed to be a Christian so I said, "I'm sorry, I just can't offer you any food for that reason."

He left fairly quickly and I wouldn't say we parted as friends. I don't think that would be quite true. He went away. However, about a year later my doorbell rang and there he was again.

He said, "You can give me lunch today."

"Why?"

He said, "I've got a job."

I replied, "You can have all the food in the house. Come on in." I was glad that he had come back.

You see, that is tough talk, isn't it? There is nothing in the Bible to say that a Christian should be a soft touch. Even looking after widows, there is some very clear guidance – rules for being sensible about it. But that is the rule there: If a man will not work, he has no right to food. Tough talk. Work is a duty, but it was also meant to be not just an action of dignity or duty, it was meant to be a delight. God intended us to find more joy in our work than in any leisure pursuit. That was his plan, and human beings got it wrong.

If what I have been telling you is true, then two things follow – implications which we need to face as Christians. Number one, laziness is a sin. It is not a sin you hear talked about much. Priests in the Catholic Church tell me it is never confessed as a sin. They hear all sorts of sins but they never hear that one. Laziness is a sin against God. If you don't believe me, read the book of Proverbs – one of the books in the Bible that was not written for women and children at all; it is entirely for men. It mentions this sin of sloth, "laziness" – a lazy man, a sluggard. It says that if that is your sin, you need to make for the nearest antheap. It says you must go and meditate on the ants. That is the cure. You go and find some ants, sit down and watch them and meditate on that. They are God's creatures too, and how they work! Go to the ant, thou sluggard, says Proverbs in the Authorized Version.

Laziness is a sin. It is a waste of what God has given you. It is wasting time, wasting effort, and there is a vivid description in one verse of Proverbs – that a lazy man is hinged to his bed. You are hinged to the bed; you just turn over and try and get a bit more rest. What a vivid description! Who says the Bible is irrelevant?

That is one negative implication, but there is another. If laziness is a sin in God's sight – in fact it is one of the Seven Deadly Sins as the Catholics have categorised them, along with pride, lust, anger, and so on – the second implication is just as serious: unemployment is an evil. Christians should be in the forefront of fighting unemployment. It is bad for a man to be unemployed and worse for a man than a woman, as I have tried to explain. I am thrilled when I hear of Christians tackling that evil. I went to a former coal mining town where the pit had closed. When that happens in a mining village, then everybody is out of work and shops close. There is a little Pentecostal church there and they said, "We're going to do something about this." There was an empty Victorian schoolhouse and they asked the council if they could borrow it and they invited unemployed men to come there for one year and be taught a new skill by one of the church members. Then, at the end of the year, the church would seek to find a job for them. Ultimately they had seventy-five men in that village at that time in that school. I went to visit this little church that invited me to preach and I couldn't find it, and I stopped at the bus stop where there was a row of people waiting for the bus, and I said, "Can you tell me where this church is?" Their faces lit up and they said, "It's a wonderful church. That church has done more for this community than anybody else." They spoke at length and were all so enthusiastic about what those Christians had done. When I got to the church I said, "I'm just thrilled to be here. I have heard so much good about you from outside, about your concern for unemployed men in this village." Well, that was just one little case. I spoke about it wherever I could – to politicians, to whoever would listen.

One of my solutions to the problem is not acceptable today: instead of paying benefits to unemployed men to do nothing, why don't we pay their wives to stay at home and look after their kids? Children under ten need their mother at home. So often she is out working and they are farmed off to some babysitter.

Men need work more than money but when I checked

statistics (some time ago now) two-thirds of the new jobs were going to women in this country. The reason was, of course, women were more suited to the jobs that were becoming available. In the Industrial Revolution, men were needed, hands were needed, muscles were needed in the factories, and male employment went right up. But in the technological revolution, women are better at it and so more jobs are going to them. They can handle a keyboard or a computer much more efficiently than men. The two fastest growing industries in this country are the service and the information industries and in both women are much better because they are much better at communicating than men. We have a rising problem with unemployment and I think it would be better for a man to be struggling to do a job and being employed and for the wife to be looking after the children than for him to be unemployed. But the taxation situation is against marriage and family life at the moment, and that needs to be spoken out against. Clearly it is bad for family and bad for society.

So unemployment is an evil and it is a major problem throughout Europe. If we cannot do anything, at least we can encourage those who can to keep in mind all the men who feel they are of no value to our community.

All this has been about work in the light of creation, but creation does not have the last word in society – the Fall does at the moment. Creation is not what it was when it left God's hands. Sin has got in. One of the first things that has been corrupted by sin is work. When Adam first sinned – led by his wife, but responsible for it – Adam was punished with work that became very much harder. Instead of plucking fruit from the trees and maybe pruning them or whatever was needed, he now had to plough the ground by the sweat of his brow. The fruit was out of his reach.

From then on, work was going to be hard. He was going

to be exhausted by it. For Eve, family relationships went wrong. A woman may go to work – there is nothing in the Bible against women working. Was this really the idea of a wife there or should this be A major role of the ideal wife in Proverbs 31 is that of a real estate agent. She made a lot of money from it, which pleased her husband. She put her family first. For a man, job first; for the wife, relationships first. That is where her life suffered, but Adam suffered in his work, and since the Fall, work is no longer what God intended it to be. It has become grinding labour. It has become something that is too much for many people – something they long to get away from, hoping for early retirement or redundancy with a golden handshake.

Secondly, work has lost its purpose. No longer has work become an end in itself, worth doing for its own sake, except for a few skilled craftsmen. For many people, work has become a means to another end – whether that is to make a lot of money or to exercise power or achieve status. It is no longer worth doing in itself and for itself. It is regarded as a stepping stone to something else; a means to achieve some other objective. God never intended that either. Sin has done that as well. Thirdly, the workplace has become somewhere where compromise seems inevitable. Unless you work for yourself, you are caught up with other sinners in a system that puts the pressure on you to do things against your conscience. In a fallen world other people don't have the same standards as you do. It is increasingly difficult even for doctors and lawyers, never mind people doing other jobs, to stick out against what their colleagues accept as normal practice, as a socially acceptable practice, but one which God says is immoral.

A girl came up to me after I had been preaching. I had happened to refer to 1 Corinthians 11, and I mentioned that in God's sight for a man to have long hair and for a woman to have short hair is a failure to acknowledge what God has made us, and, when we gather for worship, the angels look at our hairstyles, apparently. They may be at the back of the church, and they see whether we are acknowledging that we are either a man or a woman, as the case may be. The most obvious way we acknowledge that is in our hairdo. Afterwards, the young lady said: "David, what can I do? I am a hairdresser and increasingly women are coming in wanting the shortest possible hair and the men are coming in for shampoos and sets and perm waves and I don't know what else with their shoulder-length hair."

I answered, "What does your conscience say?"

She replied, "I feel guilty about doing it."

I said, "Listen, you must always do what your conscience tells you or you will lose it. It is a very delicate instrument and if we don't look after our conscience we lose it; it goes blunt. Always give your conscience the benefit of the doubt."

She went home and she gave up the business. It is not easy to be a preacher telling people to lose their business, but she did. Then she was offered another job and she came to me and said, "David there is one job that I've always longed to have in my whole life, but I wasn't fully qualified for it and I thought I could never have it and that's why I went into hairdressing. As soon as I gave up the hairdressing, I was offered the job in spite of my lack of qualifications." She remained happy in that job. I was thrilled for her sake, but she had a conscience. She knew that God did not like what she was doing, but in so many spheres today you have to do something like that. It takes a courageous man to risk his job and his income – which means taking a risk for his family too – to refuse to do what he knows is wrong in God's sight, but it is increasingly necessary. That is what sin has done to work.

It has also introduced all kinds of wrong motives to your work: greed, pride. Work has become a bit more of a competitive thing rather than a cooperative thing. If a sales representative can steal customers from another firm deliberately, it is "dog eats dog" and the motivation gets very twisted.

Finally, in a sinful world a man's value is based on his work. That is a tragedy. If I asked you, "What are you?" What would you say? Would you talk about your job? Because that is not what you *are*, it is what you *do*. In our world, the value of a man is seen as being what he *does*. What you *are* is a child of God. That is your value, but if you lose that value, what are you left with but the contribution you can make to society? What is my value to God? Is it that I travel the world, preaching and teaching? No, my value to him is that I am his child; I am his son – that is what I am. Yes, God is interested in what I do too, but what I am is not what I do. That is why some men lose their identity when they retire or when they are made redundant.

I came across a man in Oxford who was a high flyer—he did one business deal after another, but he had been made redundant three times within a very short time. He felt as if he was of no value at all, that people did not want him. Then he began to see that to God he was of value in himself. When he discovered that, he then could say, "Now God, what do You want me to do?"

God said, "I want you to minister to redundant business-men." He became official director of an Anglican ministry to redundant men – having a great life, totally fulfilled. Isn't that lovely? He had to learn that he was of value *in himself* before what he *did*. Then God put him in a job that he could do beautifully because a man who has been made redundant three times knows what it is like. He can really pick people up.

We have thought about work in the light of God's *creation*, what he intended it to be, and then about life after the Fall, when sin has spoiled it in many ways, but now I want to consider work in the light of *redemption*. We are here on earth to help to redeem it – to save it from itself, to show people what the kingdom of God can be like on earth; to give them a glimpse of God's original creational intention for us, so that they can want it again and be willing to be cleansed from their sins; so they can be what God meant them to be. We are here to be a kind of demonstration of God's original intention. How then do we redeem our daily work from Monday to Friday? In Christ it can and must be redeemed.

The first thing is to realise *why* God wants us to go to work. There are three reasons in the Bible. One: he wants us to go to work to get money. Do not be embarrassed about that. He wants us to earn our living. So that, as he says, we can support ourselves and our family, and have enough to give away to those who need it. That is the ambition to get money. Go to work to get enough money so that you and your family do not need to depend on anybody else and so that you have got a margin to give away. Too many people today actually live right up to their total income – on themselves. They get the highest mortgage they can afford and often don't think ahead to when interest rates might go up. That is when they get into the negative activity and get into debt. They have spent right up to the limit, and when demands go a little over they are finished.

A Christian does not live up to the limit of his income. He has an ambition to give away, not just to support himself – but Christians ought to support themselves. They should not live on charity, even that of other Christians. Now again I have some pretty straight things to say. People ask me sometimes, "Do you live by faith now?"

"No – or, rather, I always did."

"Oh, but you don't have a salary now from church; you don't have a regular wage?"

"No, I don't but I lived by faith when I did. I live quite

frankly on whatever I receive for the work I do."

I call that earning, and sometimes when a chairman says we are going to take a "love offering", I say: "That's not a love offering, that's my wages."

We are all on the same level in God's sight. A labourer is worthy of his hire. Jesus said when he sent out the apostles as missionaries: "Now receive what they give you" – because a labourer is worthy of his hire. I, like everybody else, must do a job that is worthy of what I receive.

This whole idea that some Christians live by faith and some don't is not biblical. In fact, if you are a small business-man today, trying to keep afloat in today's world, knowing that a Christian must never be in debt and therefore must always pay bills right on time and not wait for the last demand from the lawyer; to be obedient to God and pay every bill on time (so that he is never in debt because that is a sin in the Bible) that businessman needs far more faith than I do. When big firms don't pay him on time and wait until the last possible moment before they pay their debts, and still he needs to keep his cash flow going, that man has to have more faith in God than I do. We all have to live by faith because to be obedient to God is a costly business in this world. We all need to earn our money.

So in years of itinerant work I did not send out begging letters. I did not have churches and individuals supporting me. I lived by what I did for others. I call that earning, however it is done. Now earning is basically the duty of every able-bodied and able-minded Christian man. That is why you go to work, so that you are not on charity, so that you are not begging, so that you are not dependent on others. Or if they give you a gift, that is entirely their prerogative; that is fine. There is a place for gifts but there is a firm place for earning. That is why Paul wrote to the Corinthians and Thessalonians that: when I was with you, I gave you an example, I earned my living by working with my hands. Therefore, make it your ambition to be dependent on nobody. There it is. That is a reason to go to work. It is not the only reason but it is a good one.

Secondly, you go to work to love your neighbour. What is loving your neighbour? It is not having a nice feeling inside so that your heart speeds up every time you see them. That is not the love here, that is a kind of sentimental romantic love. According to Jesus, loving your neighbour is binding a man's wounds up when he has fallen among thieves. In other words, it is seeing a real need and meeting it. If your job is meeting the real needs of other people, you are loving your neighbour every day you go to work. You are fulfilling His commandment. I hope that gets you excited.

In that article, "Keep Mondays Special", I wrote that Christians ought to say, "Hallelujah, it's Monday morning – I'm off to love my neighbour. I'm off to serve the Lord." That is a totally different attitude to work, isn't it? If you are meeting a real need of somebody else, you are loving your neighbour. Now there are some jobs in which it might be a little difficult to prove it. I once heard of a man whose job was to take a lump of wood and grind it up to become wooden raspberry pips which were then put in a red plastic mixture, in artificial joke jam tarts – which you would put on somebody's plate and then laugh when they "broke" their teeth eating them. I must admit, I thought: could that be loving your neighbour? Is that meeting a real need?

I will tell you one job that is not loving your neighbour but is very common in the City of London: money trading, which is no more and no less than professional gambling. It is always getting money at someone else's loss without any exchange of goods or services of equal value. London has become the gambling centre of the world in money trading. It is the poorer nations that lose every time, who can't move money around quickly enough. I got into a lot of trouble for saying that when I spoke to six hundred members of the London Stock Exchange and lawyers. They asked me for a title to publicise before the meeting and I gave them this one: "You can't take it with you, and if you could it would burn." They absolutely refused to publicise that title. I had to revise it and it became: "How to invest your money beyond the grave" – because Jesus said a lot about that.

People are so concerned about piling it up for their retirement and their pension, they don't think about investing beyond the grave. The richest people in the world finish up as paupers two minutes after they are dead unless they have sent enough on ahead. Jesus told us how to lay up treasure in heaven, but that is another story. Money trading, which is simply moving around vast amounts by computers in seconds around the world, is going on all the time and I wonder how that can be loving my neighbour when I am not giving the people who I am taking the money from anything of value in return.

Let me give you some other examples of really loving your neighbour. Some years ago, there was a street sweeper in Leeds and every morning before he went to work he went into a little parish church, when they were still open. (It is now locked up.) He went in and leaned his brush and shovel against the communion rail, and he knelt down and said, "Lord, bless my work today." His streets were the cleanest in Leeds and that man was in full-time Christian service, though very few Christians would have recognised that, but he was doing a great job for the Lord.

There was a lady who was chief surgeon at a Beijing hospital. When she became a Christian, she was sacked from being a surgeon and she was told the only job she could have now as a Christian was cleaning the toilets. Now that lady, with the skilful hands of a surgeon, was cleaning toilets and she said, "I clean them as if the Lord is going to use it." She had seen it; she had got it: she was in full-time Christian service, loving her neighbour, doing a very necessary task, earning just enough to support herself.

I will never forget listening to the testimony of a Chinese man in Brighton. He had been in prison for seventeen years because he was a Christian. He was the only Christian of the wing of his prison so they gave him the worst job of all, which was to clean the sewage out from each cell. There was a hole which led to a channel into a kind of concrete cesspit – open, just a big concrete box and it all went in there. It filled up every day from the prison and he was given the job of shovelling it out into a wheelbarrow, taking it all to a field and spreading it. Because he was short, he could not reach the bottom of the cesspit with his shovel so they made him jump into it. Every morning he had to jump up to his chest in human excreta and shovel it out. You would say that was about the worst job any man could have, wouldn't you? He redeemed it. He was not allowed to pray aloud or to sing praises aloud in his cell. When he got into the cesspit, he noticed that nobody would come within two hundred metres because, as he shovelled it all, it released the stench. He thought, "I can sing here and I can pray here." He began to sing, and he learned a song from an American missionary: *I came to the garden alone while the dew was still on the roses. And he walked with me and he talked with me and he tells me I'm his own.* It was the only song, I think, he knew at first, but he would jump into this muck and start singing. Anything further removed from roses you couldn't smell.

He said, "That became the garden of Eden to me and I looked forward to it every day. The job changed." When you hear a testimony like that, you feel, "Why have I ever grumbled about work; why have I thought I have been given a rotten job?" That man was praising the Lord in it and loving his neighbour because it had to be done.

The final motive for going to work is to glorify God. You cannot do that if you do your work badly. It is concerned with the quality of work and your attitudes to your colleagues. The witness at work is not spreading texts around or necessarily telling them all about Jesus. The witness at work is that you do your work in such a way that they see it and glorify your Father who is in heaven. We had a lovely convert in the Royal Air Force. He was in the accounts department and some months later I was talking to the Wing Commander (Admin) in charge of that wing and that department. He was asking me about the church – not really interested, but he said, "How's it doing?"

I said, "We have got one of your men from your department."

He asked, "Who is that?"

I gave his name and he said, "That's the best man I've got now. He's the man I can really rely on; if a job needs doing and doing well, I go to him. If he has to stay to do overtime to finish it, he will stay. Best man I've got."

That man was witnessing at work. Whatever you do, do it in the name of Jesus. You see, it is not the boss who is going to inspect your work, it is Jesus.

I want to give you an added incentive to seeing your daily work differently. I am going to say I believe in something the early church believed in strongly for four hundred years. Augustine persuaded a church council to condemn what I am going to tell you now as heresy, and since then it virtually disappeared, but it was rediscovered about 150 years ago by one group of Christians. It is still not clearly or widely taught by the church, and it is the Millennium. In the New Testament, the Millennium means a period of a thousand years when Jesus is going to reign on this earth and show what can be done when the devil is out of it and Jesus is running it, and when the government will be Christian. The television will be in Christian hands; from the banks to the courts, it will all be in Christian hands. Is this a pipe dream? The nations will disarm multilaterally and they will not learn war any more. They will beat their swords into ploughshares and their spears into pruning hooks. It is in the Bible: there are dozens of promises not about heaven but about this old earth transformed under the right government. That thousand-year period is put *after* Jesus returns. We cannot really see the kingdom of heaven established on earth until the King gets back, but when he gets back the devil will be kicked out. That is why politicians cannot fulfil their promises today – because the devil is ruling this world, because he is the prince of this world, the god of this world, the ruler of this world and they cannot get rid of him. Neither can the church. We can release his victims, demonstrate the power of our kingdom over his, but we cannot get rid of him. That is why the world will remain in such a mess and get worse.

There is a promise of Jesus returning to reign on this world. Do you believe that Jesus is coming back? Do you believe you will come back with him? If not, why not? You see, not only is he coming back to the earth but all Christians who have died are coming back also, and not for two minutes as many Christians seem to think. I believe quite firmly that the early church was right in believing in the bodily reign of Christ on earth. To quote a bishop at that time, it was Augustine's dislike of the physical world that meant that he could not accept the idea of Jesus coming back bodily to reign physically on this old physical earth and transforming even nature so that the wolf would lie down with the lamb. The lion would eat straw like the ox. You have read that in the Bible – do you dismiss it as poetry or do you take it seriously? A world in which there will be peace at last and a world in which he will judge the nations with justice and righteousness.

The reason we cannot get peace today is that we cannot get justice. If people don't feel they have had justice, there will be no peace. That verse, "They will beat their swords into ploughshares and their spears into pruning hooks and not lift up sword against nation and neither shall they learn war anymore", is in Isaiah and Micah; it is also on the block of granite outside the United Nations Headquarters outside New York, but it is only half the verse. It is: "When the Lord reigns in Zion, he will settle the disputes between the nations and they will beat their swords into ploughshares." You cannot have half the verse, you have to have the whole thing or nothing.

I believe that when he comes back he is going to share the world government with us. We are preparing to take the world over in Jesus' name, but only when he returns. Suddenly that makes daily work altogether different.

We had a bank manager where we lived and he became a Christian. He led all his staff to the Lord and it was a joy going into the bank. They were held up by robbers at gunpoint – they were lying on the floor and robbed of five hundred thousand pounds. It hit all the headlines. The bank sent counsellors down from headquarters to counsel them through the trauma – who found themselves being counselled! I spoke to the bank manager and told him, "You know, all the banks are going to be in Christian hands one day. Jesus said if you are faithful in looking after other people's money I will give you a lot of your own to look after." If you are faithful in small amounts of money, he will give you large amounts – entrusting you with them. He may well say to you: "Well done, good and faithful servant, I'll put you in charge of ten cities." Why not? Do you really believe this?

I had to write a little book because the church is in such confusion about the Millennium that all they could think of was the year 2000, which God was not celebrating at all; it was not even in his diary. I wrote a book *Hope for the Millennium*, which looked at six different theories that were in the church. Now when Christians disagree about something they agree on a conspiracy of silence not to mention it at all. It has happened with baptism: "You mustn't mention this. Let's all be united and let's all stay together, don't bring up things we disagree about." Well, you have heard about amillennial, pre-millennial, post-millennial, but have you heard of all of them? A friend says, "That is a pre-posterous question!". There are people who now say "I'm pan-millennial" – meaning that things will pan out all right in the end.

I believe we have lost one of the greatest hopes of the future. Most Christians that I have talked to have a hope for another world—they have no hope for this one. I have a hope for this world that Jesus is coming back to reign. I used to sing a song when I was a boy – I didn't really understand it then, but it had a lovely tune and I loved this song: *Sing we the King who is coming to reign; glory to Jesus the Lamb that was slain. Life and salvation his empire shall bring; Joy to the nations when Jesus is King.* Now I understand that, and I look forward to the Millennium, even before the new heaven and the new earth. This old earth is going to see what it will really be like under Jesus' government.

A man came up to me after a service and said, "David, for the first time I can relate my faith to my job."

I asked, "How? What's your job?"

He explained: "I am in charge of de-polluting the rivers of England. We're achieving it and even have salmon coming up the Thames. I know that in Revelation even the oceans are going to be polluted before the end and they already are.

When Jesus comes back he will be looking for someone to de-pollute the rivers, won't he? I want that job. I am going to study all I can about that."

If your hope is just looking forward to going to heaven and singing choruses one after another forever, what's that to do with your daily job? But if you are going to be running this world with Jesus, if there will be nothing on the television that he can't watch, if there will be nothing published in magazines that he can't read and look at, he is going to need people to do all this. That is why Paul, writing to the Corinthians, said, "I hear some of you are taking other Christians before an unbelieving judge and suing them in court. How dare you when you are going to judge the nations."

You had better learn now how to run this world properly because you are going to be doing it when Christ comes. What a motivation!

4

MAKING DISCIPLES

The key to meetings for men is this: if a meeting has to be supported by men, it will not survive. If a meeting supports men, they will keep on coming. So the big question is this: is what we are doing for men something that they have to support, or something that is supporting them? If it really is supporting them, they will want it and want it regularly because they will need it. So everything will boil down to whether men feel they need what is being offered to them. Most churches don't do anything special for men at all. This is partly because it is more difficult – men are very busy and tied up. But that is not the only reason. I find a complete lack of faith in so many churches: "Well, our church couldn't do anything like that for men."

Of course, if you don't do anything for men you are not going to get them. It is as simple as that. They don't drop out of the sky. "We're praying for more men in our church." My response to that is: stop praying and start discipling. They don't come into the church in answer to prayer, they come into the church because you are reaching out to them and giving them something that they find they need and not just want.

Jesus didn't start the church for Sunday schools or women's meetings, so what did he do and how can we do it? I want to be very practical. I want to commend to you a discipling programme for men that I believe any church could develop and run successfully. I went to a church in

Cornwall and I counted up the women to men ratio and it was two to one. I said to the pastor, "The one thing I can tell you about your church without knowing your church is that you don't have anything for men on their own."

He replied, "No, we don't."

I said: "Well, look at the result in your congregation; you can see it."

I can tell as soon as I go into a congregation whether the men are being discipled or not, or whether they are just attending with their wives.

What kind of programme do I mean? I don't mean men's breakfasts with speakers. That is a good start, but it won't see them through. It is essentially an outreach to get men together to get them to know each other. I heard about a church with a fireside men's football team – that's a start, it gets men related and gets them friendly, knowing each other. But that is not discipling them. You want to take them much further. Obviously, I mean getting the men together, and my suggestion is that if you are going to disciple them properly you need a minimum of once a month. You may develop more than that but it is better to increase than decrease the frequency. But a minimum if you are really going to be serious is a monthly meeting. Then you have got to decide when that is going to be. It may mean that a church has to have more than one because some men are on shift work and need to have a men's group that meets on a different day every week.

You have got to find out when the men of your church are available, and it may not all be at the same time. On the whole, a good start is early Saturday morning. Many churches start with that, at least with an initial group. Then they develop other groups. I know groups that meet at five o'clock on Thursday morning. I know a group that meets on Sunday evening after the children are all in bed. You have got to find a time when the men can get together for at least one hour, but preferably an hour and a half, once a month.

When you are starting up, may I urge you to ask for a commitment rather than an interest? I mean by an "interest" this: "We are going to start a men's group here. All men are warmly invited. I'm sure you'll have a warm welcome if you can come along." Don't start that way – that is *by invitation*. Start by *commitment* – by saying: "We are starting a men's discipling group, and we invite those men who are willing to commit themselves to come for six months, to six monthly meetings unless unavoidably detained by emergency or unexpected demand." The reason is that you cannot in less than six months build up a true discipling group. It does take time. If you just invite all the men they will all come the first time, half of them will come to the second, a quarter for the third, and there will be a diminishing response. They came because they were curious or just interested.

It is better to start with four men who will say, "I will come for six months," and give it a serious trial. That is a serious commitment. If you do it properly, after six months you won't keep them away, but it does require that kind of continuity to get it properly going. It is better to start with a few who are committed rather than a lot who are merely interested or curious. You will need a bunch of men in your church who say, "I'm willing to try it once a month. That's the time I can manage, and I'll promise to come every month for six months unless I cannot because something else too urgent, too much of an emergency claims my time."

You have got a group of people. There are six items to be covered in a discipling group. You may not cover all six in each meeting. But you need to ring the changes with six activities. I am not giving you these six in any order of priority; I am just telling you the six things I see men doing together in such a group. Worship undoubtedly is going to take some part, where men can learn to praise and pray aloud together. That is going to take time, and worship for men will be a little different from mixed worship. Most of the choruses today are not masculine choruses. I don't want to be cynical, but I wouldn't expect a bunch of working men to sing the chorus, "I sing you a love song, a love song to Jesus." It just isn't the place to begin. "It is God who trains my arms for battle" – do you know that one? I think the guitar is not a masculine instrument. Men like a brass band or an accordion. I have known tremendous men's worship with just a trombone: strong music; strong content and words.

Men want something to get their teeth into; something they can think about when they are singing. Merely repetitive "I love you" is not natural to men. Choosing the worship, it is wonderful to hear men really letting go – and men who are too shy to open their mouths, especially if they can't sing in tune in front of their families – in a bunch of men. We had a "Men for God" meeting in Dudley Town Hall, six hundred men came, we had a couple of trombones, and we began that day by singing "How Great Thou Art". I could not hear myself sing, even though I was singing at the top of my voice.

They told me that right out on the High Street people stopped and listened. Six hundred men at full blast! I leave you to imagine. It was a foretaste of heaven. The men were learning to let themselves go and praise because none of them could hear themselves. But they were contributing to it. For prayer, it is vital that those men who pray long prayers be shut up. Often with a bunch of men I say, "Sit in a circle. Pray around the circle and no more than two sentences at the most for each of you. You can come back for a second go later." That way each man can freely get two sentences out and often they are so real and meaningful instead of these long, rambling prayers full of clichés.

It means everybody is learning to get it out and people are taking part in a prayer meeting. Worship, encouraging male worship together, singing together, praying together, takes time. The best worship leader I knew in Britain was a farmer who played the accordion. When he had finished leading the worship he literally melted – you could see it running all down him, with his great big accordion. He was so praising the Lord that men could not resist it, and they joined in. If you have such an accordionist or trombone player, grab them and use them. Offer the Lord strong worship. That is number one.

Number two: teaching is obviously going to be part of it but don't let the pastor monopolise the teaching. Often men in the group have much more to teach on certain aspects of work, money, sex and so on. Ring the changes and the teaching does not need to be an hour. It can be five minutes. "What have you learned from your job about being a Christian? Share it with us." Teaching is not just lecturing it is training, helping people to do it. That kind of teaching, is a vital part, but I'll come back to that.

Ministry is the third thing, and this is the key. Once you get into this, the men find that this is a meeting that supports them and not just a meeting they support. That is the breakthrough moment because then it will become a priority for men. I will tell you about a church in Cornwall. I met the pastor two years later and he said, "David, you gave us some problems." I said, "What problems?" He said, "We have got two problems we never had before you came."

"What are they?" I asked.

"One, we've got more men than women in the church now. We don't know how to handle it. Two, we have far too many leaders in the church now."

"Aren't you happy with those problems?"

He said, "We're very happy, but they are new, and we're

not used to them."

I replied, "When you've got too many leaders that's the time to plant new churches. Far too many start new churches with members, but you don't do it that way – you grow the church by multiplying your leaders. Then you will find the members who will grow automatically. But if you grow your members without growing the leaders, the leaders are going to be stretched and have burn out. I've seen that happen. Multiply your leaders. That's the way to grow and you only do that by discipling men." That is how Jesus did it and that's how we do it. Mutual ministry—this is what I mean. You break your men up into small groups—three or four in each group. Then you encourage them to minister to each other.

Now how do you do that? You do it by encouraging them to be frank with one another and ask each other questions.

"What's the greatest problem that you're going to face in the next month before we meet again?"

"Well, I've got a difficult interview with my boss on Thursday."

"Right, let's pray about that."

Simple, isn't it?

"What's your biggest temptation at work?"

"Well, it's this: to be honest."

"Let's talk about it."

"Right, let's all pray about this problem."

It may sound naïve but you wouldn't believe what results I have had. Now this is why you have got to have the six-month commitment because men are not going to reveal these things to each other until they have got to know each other and trust each other and know that it won't be gossiped about back home. You may not be able to do it the first time you meet, but that is your objective, to get to the point where men will talk to each other frankly and minister to each other.

I can give you one or two examples: I met a Church of

Scotland minister at a conference in London. Everybody called him Sandy. Alexander was his real name. Sandy was grumbling to me. He was a minister in a little village called Auldene, you have probably never heard of, near Inverness. He said, "David, nobody will come up and help me with my ministry. I've asked preachers from down south to come but they all say it's too far. It's quite depressing. Nobody will come and do anything for us in our little village."

I said, "I'll come, Sandy."

He said, "No, you won't. I know people who have promised, and then they never did."

I said, "Sandy, you're not listening; I'll come."

He said, "You won't, will you?"

Again I said, "I'll come."

He replied, "I don't like to ask you."

It just became more depressing. I said, "Sandy, I'll come for a whole week. Now did you hear that?" He finally believed it. I continued: "But on one condition: that at least one night, the Tuesday or Wednesday, is for men only."

He said, "Fine, I'll book the telephone kiosk on the village green for that."

I said, "Why? How many men have you got in the church?"

He said, "None. They're all old women."

Mind you, I wasn't getting blessed by what he was telling me now, but I had made a promise, and if I make a promise I keep it. So I went up there, and he had actually booked a little village hall for the Tuesday evening men's meeting. He said, "I think it's only going to be the two of us, David."

I answered, "Never mind, that's a men's meeting. Where's your faith?"

About ten past seven a man came walking down the village street and approached the village hall. Sandy said, "Hey! Somebody's come!" Then another came. Then a car drew up. By the end, he was out in the street dancing for joy. Forty men had come. He said none would, but forty did.

Our lack of faith is often a root, the root problem. They came, forty men. I decided actually to take a risk that time and treat them as if they were a discipling group. I split them into groups of four and said, "Ask each other some of these questions and start ministering to each other." A bit of a risk but never mind. I found myself in a group of four, one of whom was a giant of a man with fair hair, blue eyes—he looked like a Viking and in fact proved to be a Norwegian living up there. I said to him, "What's the biggest problem you've got with your job?"

He blushed crimson and said, "I don't like to tell you."

"Go on. Tell me. Don't be afraid."

He said, "My biggest problem is loneliness."

"Why? What's your job?"

"I'm a deep sea diver in the North Sea on the oil rigs. I weld the legs of the rigs where they crack. I work alone in darkness, welding the legs of the North Sea rigs. I feel all alone. I can't even feel that God is down there and I am a Christian. I can't even pray down there when I go down into that darkness. I feel I've left life up on the surface. It's desperate. I don't know how much longer I can do it; if it wasn't for the money I wouldn't go on."

I said, "When do you go down next?"

"Thursday morning."

I said to the other two in the little group, "Thursday morning, you've got a job. We're going to pray that man down into the North Sea," and we did.

I have not met him since but I had the loveliest letter from him. He wrote and said that on Thursday he went down, and inside his diving helmet he started singing to the Lord and he said, "I had such a wonderful time with the Lord at the bottom of the North Sea. Suddenly it has changed my job altogether. I can't describe the difference it has made." He is no longer lonely. However, that man might that man might still be struggling with that problem had he not had a chance to get the help of the little bunch of men around him.

I think of another man, a sales representative. He used to spend nights in dingy hotels in backstreets of cities. It was all he could afford. He was hawking around something for sale that wasn't terribly expensive. That was his life and he said, "When I'm away from home in these dingy hotels, I'm lonely. I'm away from my wife. It is always in the area where the girls are. They come into the hotel looking for customers and the hotel doesn't object. It gives them rooms. It's a real temptation. I've had a real fight. I haven't given in yet but I have a horrible feeling I will one day because they're pretty girls and they're available. I'm on my own."

So the next time he went a little group prayed for him. He was sitting alone in the hotel lounge when two girls of the street came in. They looked all around the lounge, and one said to the other, "There's nobody here," and off they went, and he was sitting right in front of them. He said, "The Lord blinded their eyes; they never saw me." He said, "Now I know that wherever I am the Lord is there." That solved the problem for him. This is what happens when men become willing to share that kind of thing and say, "Pray for me," or "Can you advise me?" When a man's got into financial problems, is there another man in the fellowship who could help him do a bit of budgeting and help him to get out of that problem? There is nowhere to turn. His bank manager just wants the overdraft back and nobody else is willing to help. What a difference it can make if a man in that church who can handle finance says, "Let's go and look at your budget and let's help you to find out where you could be saving a bit and how you could get on top of this." That man is not going to say, "Oh dear, there's another men's meeting I've got to go to. Pastor is begging me to support it." That man will say, "I'm going to be there next month. That's seen me through one month. I must be there." Do you see what I mean? It becomes a self-supporting brotherhood that men need and want. It transforms them; it really does. That is what I mean by mutual ministry. You need to build up the relationships before you can really do that. I was taking a risk doing it in a public meeting in Inverness where the men didn't know each other. Nevertheless, it did show them what can be done. That is miles away from turning up for breakfast to listen to a speaker. It is really getting to grips with the man's need where he is. To men, that is the very heart of a men's discipling group.

Fourthly, and this may surprise you: fun. Men need to let their hair down with each other. They need to be pals together. They need to be friends as well as brothers. They need to have fun together. Go ten-pin bowling for the evening; five-a side-football. There is a place for that sort of thing. If it is the only thing in the discipling programme then it is totally inadequate. Yes, for their fun they can bring their wives if it is something that their wives can join in with. Let them go fishing together. Most of them can't do it, and the ones who know how can teach the others how to do it. Mind you, fishing is not necessarily fun. I saw a cartoon where a wife was sitting in the back of a rowing boat under an umbrella while her husband was fishing in the middle of a lake, and she was saying, "I haven't had such fun since I cleaned the oven."

Number five: working with your hands together. Doing a bit of manual work. It is amazing what that does. I design two or three church buildings a year, and there is one in a place called Tamworth. The church built it themselves. They spent six hundred thousand pounds but it had to be insured for two-and-a-half million. They did a magnificent job. You would not believe it had been built by amateurs. The pastor learned bricklaying. They had so much given to them. All the breeze blocks were given to them because they were chipped or faulty. (They were seconds at the local factory making them.) All their hardcore was dumped on the site for them.

Those men working together were a brotherhood. There were men there who might have had a huge salary, but they could not knock a nail in straight; they had to be shown how. It is a very good leveller, but there is something about working with your hands that is healthy – and working with your hands together and being taught how to do it by someone who can do it – there is something about that. Decorating the church hall, digging a pensioner's garden. You can find something, but from time to time a discipling group should get their hands dirty together. Do something very practical — it works wonders.

Sixth and finally, reaching out to men. The men out there do not think the church is for men. It does not have the right image for men. But when they come along they are impressed with the fact that here is a bunch of men who mean business with the Lord; men who are serious about the Christian faith and life. Nothing makes a bigger impression on men than seeing a bunch of men interested in the faith. A church that has a men's group is in a unique place to win men, to bring men into a male setting where they are going to feel at home – men like themselves but who have that extra.

Those are the six things that we need to include, but not every time. Ring the changes. A bit of variety is the spice of life.

I want to go back to the teaching. I want to give you a kind of curriculum or agenda of the kind of thing that needs to be taught. Talking to men I am to talk in down-to-earth terms about things that I would find difficult to say in a family service. Men need to hear about the kinds of things in this book but they won't unless there is an all-male context in which they can be spoken to directly. Men can go to church for years and never be talked to about the vital things in their life: sex, work, money (how to get it, how to save it, how to spend it). We need to know what the Bible says about all these things. We need a male context in which we can speak frankly and honestly together about these things.

Let me give you a curriculum or agenda for the teaching to cover – maybe over two or three years, or whatever. Part of it I list under the title of "responsibilities" and part I list under the title of "motives". Men need not only to be taught what to do but how and why to do it. I have learned that you can preach until you are blue in the face about what people ought to do, but until they are motivated and want to do it, not much is going to happen.

Let us look first at the responsibilities. I never talk about men's "rights" – that is the word everybody is using today. Thomas Paine (born in Thetford, Norfolk) wrote a book entitled *Rights of Man*, which immediately got a woman in Paris writing a book *The Rights of Women*. Both books have been incorporated into the United Nations Charter. The Declaration of Human Rights has picked up those documents from the eighteenth century, incorporated them, and now "rights" is the word everywhere. We demand our rights. We have a right to a job. We have a right to happiness. We have a right to money. Well, we don't! In the kingdom of heaven nobody has any rights. The one thing we don't talk about in a men's discipling course is your rights. We do talk about your responsibilities. What are they?

Number one: there is a man's responsibility for himself. A man is responsible for himself before God. I have seen many criminals through courts. I have got many of them off – not by pleading they were irresponsible but by pleading they were responsible for themselves. In courts I have heard it so often: the psychiatrist pleads that the man was not responsible – that because of his upbringing, his heredity or environment, he could not help it. So he is put on probation. I have often spoken to criminals and I have covered the front page of a newspaper with one of the defences I made for a murderer and got them off. Not because they didn't have a hand in it but because I told them: "Be a man; take responsibility for yourself. Say, 'Yes, your honour, I did it, and I chose to do it.'"

This takes judges by such surprise they do not quite know how to handle it. They are so used to hearing excuses and all sorts of things, but I say, "You are a man under God, and you are what you are because you chose to be what you have become." Our character is the result of our own choices, whatever start in life we had. We chose the friends we had. We chose the things we did with them. We have made choices that have made us what we are now. Therefore, I am responsible for what I am now, and so are you. I have taught criminals to do that and I told them in a top security jail where I spoke regularly – where an entire wing of the prison became Christian. The Governor could not understand what was going on. The prisoners broke down the walls between the cells and lived together as a caring Christian community. I could talk to them for two-and-a-half hours non-stop and they were just drinking it in. These were murderers. They were all lifers. There were drug barons. I said: "You are responsible for what you have become." We are responsible for ourselves.

Let's look at that more deeply. A man is responsible for the state of his body. God gave you that body, and it is the only body you have. You are responsible to him for how you look after it. You can dig your grave with a knife and fork if you choose. It is why smoking is something there is a big question mark about, because a Christian says, "This body is a temple of the Holy Spirit and I have made it filthy and smelly. I have exposed it to the risk of being destroyed." Is that being responsible? I am responsible for the state of my body so that it serves me. Some men look after their motorbikes and cars better than their bodies. You can get another car; you won't get another body. It is meant to serve you a good seventy years.

I am responsible for the state of my mind. Your mind is what you become. As a man thinks in his heart, so is he. You can fill your mind with all the junk that the mass media wants you to fill it with, and it becomes an attic full of rubbish. Or you can furnish it and live in it. You cannot read all the books, you cannot see all the films; you have to choose. Your choice will determine the colour of your thinking. A man is responsible for the state of his mind, and since many of our temptations come from our state of mind it is usually due to what we fed it with earlier. Many men are an accident waiting to happen because they have already done it in fantasy and in their thinking. When the circumstances are right, they will do it because their thinking has already preceded it. That is why Jesus said that is where murder and adultery begin. Thinking about it has started to do it for you. A man is responsible for what goes into his mind – what he thinks about.

A man is responsible for the state of his conscience. It is a delicate instrument. We are born with a conscience that will be conditioned by our upbringing and it will have to be revised so that it feels guilty not just when you are doing something your parents told you not to do, but when you are doing something God does not want you to do. That involves processes of educating your conscience. I was brought up in a fairly strict home that forbade bicycles, cameras and toys on a Sunday. I was brought up to believe that it was sinful to touch any of those things on a Sunday. I know now that that was what my parents thought and it is not what God thinks. When I had to cycle to church from the farm, I was in a real tizz with my conscience. "I'm cycling on a Sunday to get to church!" I've now revised my conscience and many things that I thought were wrong I no longer think are wrong. I know I am free to do them. Other things that I thought I was free to do I now know are wrong. That is because my conscience is gradually becoming more educated to the Lord than to my environment. I am responsible for the state of my conscience. Every time I go against it, it blunts its edge.

You can sear your conscience until it no longer speaks. It then whispers, and finally it goes silent. I am responsible for that. I am responsible for the state of my emotions. The church is desperately short of angry men. It is not that men in the church are not angry, but they are usually angry for the wrong reason, in the wrong place, at the wrong time with the wrong person. Otherwise, it is okay. Jesus was angry. He cleansed the temple single-handedly through sheer anger. He was angry when he was criticised for healing a man on the Sabbath. He was angry when children were kept away from him. We need to study the Lord's anger because when he comes back a second time, he is going to be angry. There will be people praying that the mountains will cover them.

The problem is not anger. The problem is that we are angry in the wrong way. If only men in church were as angry as Jesus was with the right things. You would get things happening. But since our anger is usually wrongly directed we have none left to direct rightly. Anger is a powerful thing; it can destroy good things but it can also destroy evil things. We need it. Men need emotion. They need to learn to weep. Again, many men have said to me that when they got filled with the Holy Spirit they began to cry again for the first time since they were little boys. Jesus was a real man and he wept, publicly when his heart was broken. We need to learn to weep again. I am afraid the English idea of manhood is you don't wear your heart on your sleeve. Keep a stiff upper lip and you will be admired. If you don't weep, that is not being like Jesus. Again, we weep at the wrong things. We need to weep over what he weeps over. A man is responsible for the state of his emotions and for the state of his soul.

We will never be men of God unless we are soaked in the Bible. If nothing goes into your mind but what you hear and see in the news media, you will never be a man of God. The only way to think like God and to have a mind like God is to soak yourself in his Word. There is no shortcut, and yet many men hardly look at the Bible. I made the videos entitled *Unlocking the Bible* to encourage people to get back into the Bible with excitement and understanding.

That is all the responsibility for themselves that men need to be taught. Secondly, there is the responsibility for their family—for the wife, particularly. If you want your wife to treat you like a king, there is a very simple way: treat her like a queen. We need to learn how to do that, how to look after our wives. Men need to teach each other how they have learned – sometimes the hard way, through ignorance – just how to be responsible for their wife and for their children. The average father in Britain, it was revealed some time ago, spent fifteen minutes per week with his children. I mean quality time, devoting his whole attention to the children so they have the exclusive attention and affection of the father. Fifteen minutes out of 168 hours—that has been the state of fatherhood in Britain. I want to add a particular word here: we need to know that in the teen years the father is as needed by the girls as by the boys.

Under ten the need is for a mother, but in the teens not only do boys need a father so they know what manhood is, but girls need a father too. If they don't have a father's attention they are far more likely to make a bad marriage because they will rush off after the first boy who takes them out. If they have got a good relationship with their father during their teens, the girls will have a standard of manhood that they will want to wait for.

I was talking to a girl from South Africa and she told me how much she enjoyed as well as admired her dad. She wanted a man like him, to be a good husband – not a replica of him, but she knew what a good husband was like from her relationship with her father. Girls with a bad relationship with their dad during their teen years will rush into bad marriages. That is a simplification but it is widely true. So, we need to be aware of the responsibility for our family.

There is responsibility, too, for the church to which we belong. Don't leave it to the pastor or the elders or the vicar or the PCC. Take responsibility for your church. The way to do that is just to take it. If you see something that needs doing, do it. If the chairs need putting out or stacking up, do it. Just take responsibility. I tell you the reward: you will be given more responsibility. As soon as the church sees that you can be responsible, you will get it – probably too much. But at least if you go to a church, don't just go home and have roast preacher for lunch. Don't go home and say, "What a mess our church is in." Say, "What could I take responsibility for? I'm going to do something to change our church."

You might think: why can't we have a men's group in the church? Go to your leaders and say, "We want a men's group." Don't wait for them to do it, say, "We can begin to meet together immediately." Why not? Let us go ahead and do it. Let us take responsibility so that there is a men's group in our church. If you wait for the leaders to do it, they will have already got their plates full of so much that they will put it on the agenda and it might never come off there. Take responsibility. What is to stop you and a bunch of men from meeting together? Nothing at all.

Of course, you might run into what is a common problem: that the vicar or pastor wants things under his control. It is an insecurity basically, but it is there and I know it. I have faced the temptation myself as a pastor—we want to know what is going on and we like to feel we are there, in everything. You may have a pastor or vicar like that – I hope not. But why should he stop you doing what the Lord wants you to do? You get on and do it. Take responsibility for your church.

Finally, take responsibility for your society. In a democracy we are all responsible. Our vote gives us a sense of responsibility. It is a small thing and yet it adds up. I was talking to a bunch of men in Basingstoke and one man said, after he listened to me, "I'm going to get on our local council. I don't know if there's a Christian on it but I'm determined to get at least one Christian on it." He went ahead and got on the council in order to help make Basingstoke a better city. He was talking responsibility.

Ninety percent, at least, of all the decisions that shape our society are made by men, not women. Whether the feminists like that or not, it is a fact. There has never been any society in the whole of history in which most of the major decisions were not made by men. It will continue to be that way, believe me. You might pack the House of Commons with women but the decisions will be made by men for the most part. Yet Christian men shy away from local and national politics as a dirty business. Well, get your hands dirty and get into it. I preached in Solihull and there was a black man in the congregation and his ambition was to help to change England. His name was John Taylor. I think he was badly advised to try to be an MP from Cheltenham. Anyway, he was turned down, but now he is Baron Taylor of Warwick. He is in the House of Lords, and there he is wanting to help to make the decisions. He did get in there even though he did not get into the Commons, but he had ambition.

I remember meeting him one morning and praying that he would get into Parliament. He had an ambition to make this country a better place, and he went for it. That is the kind of man who is going to get a big responsibility in the Millennium. A Christian doesn't hope to bring in the kingdom of God on earth just through getting into politics. A Christian does not have outlandish or naïve optimism about the future of this world until Jesus gets back. He knows that then it is really going to change, but he wants to get in practice now and learn how to be just and merciful now so that he can be when he is given more responsibility then. That is on the responsibility side.

Finally, *motivation*. Here are the four motivations that need to be covered in a men's discipling group.

First: the motive for Christian living is fear of God. Most men today don't fear God; they fear redundancy. They might fear illness and all kinds of things. I am talking about inside the church as well as outside. The fear of God is the beginning of wisdom. If you want to be a wise man, read the Bible. The book of Proverbs is the best book for a man to read. Billy Graham told me that he read Proverbs once a month. That is what kept him out of trouble because he was one of the few televangelists who was not caught out with a prostitute. One of the things he told me was, "I never get into a car with a woman other than my wife or daughter. If a woman offers to drive me somewhere, I take a train or a bus or a plane. I will never get in a car with a woman by herself." That is wisdom. He got it because, as he said, he reads the book of Proverbs once a month. You try that. It will make you a wise man – not necessarily a wealthy man nor a clever man but a wise man, which is what you really want to be. A wise man will make the most of life. A clever man may make a lot of money but he will finish up without it. Be wise. The fear of God is the beginning of wisdom and there is as much about fearing God in the New Testament as in the Old. Don't fool yourself. "Work out your salvation," says Paul, "with fear and trembling." What is there to fear with God? Everything. He is a holy God who loves sinners but he hates sin. If we hold on to sin and won't let go of it then he has to hate us because we have identified with it. We have made it part of us and we are not willing to let it go. We know what happens in the end when you are under the wrath of God. God can be very angry. He is very angry against sin because it hurts yourself and other people and him when we abuse his creation, what he has given to us. And he is angry. One day that anger will boil over. There is a day of anger coming. His anger with this world is going to boil over. It is already visibly obvious that his anger is resting on England.

You read Romans 1 and find out what happens to society when God is angry with it. If I tell you that homosexuality increases, and if I tell you that children become more disobedient to parents, those are only two of about thirty things in Romans 1 that are evidenced when God is angry with a society or a community. When you read your newspapers it is like reading Romans 1. God is angry with this country. But his anger at the moment is simmering. There are two words in the New Testament for God's anger: simmering and boiling over. When milk in a pan is simmering on a stove you may not get anxious, but suddenly without warning it boils over, doesn't it? Then you smell it and you rush to take it off the stove. The two words for God's anger are his simmering anger and his boiling-over anger. His simmering anger is spread over quite some time and we are already experiencing that. England needs to be told about that.

One day it is going to boil over and that is the thing to

fear. It is the fear of having preached to others and then being disqualified yourself. It is the fear, quite simply, of losing your salvation. Now, ninety-five per cent of the Christians of this country have been told: "once saved, always saved; once you have got your ticket to heaven it doesn't matter what you do, you're okay." I was so burdened by that when I met Christians living in deliberate and willful sin that I had to write a book *Once Saved, Always Saved?* The question mark in the title is important. I looked at eighty passages in the New Testament which tell you that you need to go on trusting and obeying until the end. I came to the firm conclusion through studying those eighty passages from every writer in the New Testament that we are to hold on until the end; that unless we abide or stay in the True Vine we will be cut out and burned.

When I wrote the book *The Road to Hell* many were shocked by this teaching, and I had many letters saying, "I can't believe it." I pointed out that all but two of Jesus' warnings about hell were given to born-again believers, and the two were given to Pharisees. He hardly ever talked to sinners about hell but he talked to believers about it. Many people wrote to me and said: "I couldn't believe what you said until I checked you out and it's right." That is why I wrote the book. I fear hell, and that is why I can preach it. I think it is utterly offensive for a preacher to say, "I'm going to heaven and you're going to hell." But I can preach on hell because I fear going there myself even though I am a believer. I find the fear of God is very much related to this: your security does not lie in a decision you made for Christ twenty years ago, it lies in your relationship with the Lord now. If that is right, you have an assurance that you are on your way to heaven. If that goes wrong, the first thing you lose is your assurance. I don't wake up in the morning wondering whether I'm going to heaven or not. If I am walking with the Lord and I am right with him, I know that all I have to do is keep on this road and I am right there. But I fear him.

The book of Revelation finally convinced me about it and if you have read my book *When Jesus Returns* you may recall that I point out that at the very end, when the new heaven and the new earth comes down, the word comes from the Lord: "Those who overcome will inherit all this but the cowardly and the immoral and the deceitful, liars, will be thrown into the Lake of Fire." Now when Christians read that they think that last bit is about everybody else out there. No, it isn't. The book of Revelation is entirely for Christians; it is written for seven churches and it is saying: those of you believers who overcome will inherit all this, but if you are cowardly or immoral, if you are not overcoming, then the Lake of Fire is for you. That brings the fear of the Lord back. It is not a phobia; it doesn't paralyse you. It is a very healthy thing. You become more afraid of grieving God and upsetting God than of upsetting people. That is a great step forward. It does not make you any more popular, but gaining the fear of God is a great step forward in your Christian life.

Secondly, the name of Jesus. There is power in the name of Jesus but men are embarrassed to use it. They even find it easier to talk about the Lord. That sounds a bit more respectable but the power is not in the word "Lord", it is in the name Jesus. The more often the name Jesus is on a man's lips the more he will be motivated – that is an amazing thing. A friend of mine was in the factory urinal doing his usual, standing next to another man, and this man was talking to yet another man in the next little thing. He was saying, "Christ, we've had a rough time this morning in our part of the shop. Jesus Christ, you should've heard what they. . ." and this Christian stood there and quietly said: "Would you mind not talking about him like that, about my best friend?" That was what he said. He said it very gently and very firmly. He then told him that Jesus was his best friend. Talking about Jesus does something for a man's Christian motivation, makes it much more personal than just "the Lord". I don't know why, but there is power in the name of Jesus. I have never managed to heal anybody by saying "The Lord" but with the name of Jesus I have seen wonderful things happen.

The fear of the Lord, the name of Jesus – then, thirdly, the power of the Spirit. I have hinted at this from time to time in this book, but men need to know they have been filled with the power of the Holy Spirit. They need to know they have been baptised in the Spirit. I don't hesitate to use that phrase because John the Baptist and Jesus after him used it continually many, many times. If you don't believe me, read my little book, *Jesus Baptises in One Holy Spirit*. I am not selling books, I am just telling you that if you really want to check me out, get the book. Jesus is the Baptiser.

When did you last hear that title preached about? He doesn't baptise you in water though, I can do that for you, but I can't baptise you in His Spirit. When a man is baptised in Spirit, he has got power. Most unlikely power. I think of my friend Bill. Bill was a millionaire by the age of thirty but he was ruthless in his business methods. He drove his wife to drink and his son of eighteen so hated him that he ran away from home. Then Bill met the Lord Jesus. He saw Jesus heal a person in his own sitting room and he knew that Jesus must be real to do that. He just saw it happen in his sitting room in the name of Jesus and he surrendered to Jesus that day. I went for a walk with Bill. He has a huge ocean-going yacht and he took me out into the Pacific Ocean. We landed on a Pacific island. We went for a walk on the beach. He pulled out of his pocket a piece of paper and he said, "That is the most valuable possession of mine." He said, "It's a letter from my son." He said, "I carry it next to my heart." He said,

"My boy wrote a letter to me months after he left home. My boy said, 'I met Jesus and I'm coming home." And he said, "We met in Christ." He said, "All my millions couldn't buy that letter." And Bill is now known worldwide.

Have you heard of the name Bill Subritzky? That man had a ministry of healing people and delivering people worldwide. But the first thing that he did after his conversion was to set his alarm clock for one hour earlier in the morning and from then on he read the Bible for one hour a day before he went off to work. He read it through every few months without any short cuts. He became a man of God, known the world over for power. Not the kind of financial power or the kind of push he had in business, which he certainly had as well as being a clever lawyer. He was New Zealand's biggest building contractor and one of their best-known lawyers — he was powerful, but in a destructive way. He became a powerful man for God and one of the most humble men I have ever met.

I'll tell you about one other man in Australia. Peter Bettson has distributed five hundred thousand of my tapes over the whole of Australia and into Burma and China. He came to Christ, listened to the tapes, learned more about Jesus and he just said, "I want everybody to hear the truth." He became known as the honest used-car dealer. He used to auction second-hand cars every fifty seconds on Tuesday and Thursday, not to the public but to the car dealers and that is quick business. The day after he was converted he got up at his auctioneer's desk and he said, "Well fellas, get this quick and get it straight." He said, "I'm a Christian this morning." He said, "From now on I'll tell you the whole truth about every car I sell you." A car came and he said, "It looks good but it's rotten in the chassis." He said, "I wouldn't touch it." None of them believed him. They never did so they bought it. He said, "No more bids off the wall," which means pretending to get bids when they're not coming and running a man up—you know the kind of thing.

It is illegal, it is immoral, but on TV, a leading auctioneer in this country said, "That's how you do it. You pretend a bidder over there is bidding against him." He said, "You run him up." It is illegal. It is immoral. He stopped doing it. They said, "You'll be out of business in six weeks." But he became a millionaire. And he spent the money buying tapes and walking the streets of Brisbane at night picking up drunks, looking after them. He was a real Aussie, hard-swearing, hard-drinking, and above all, hard-driving. That's Peter. Now if I drive with him, in a huge Mercedes all over Australia, when we're out in the bush two hundred miles from anywhere, he's driving at ninety-nine kilometres an hour because there was a 100 kilometre an hour limit in Australia. He drove at fifty-nine in the town, exactly, and it is a big car with a big engine. I couldn't help noticing it. I commented on it, but soon wished I hadn't.

He said, "Isn't that holiness, David?" He said, "How can I expect the angels to protect me when I'm breaking the laws made for my safety?" There's no answer to that, is there? That is the kind of man he became. Straight as a die. Then he healed not just people, he healed vineyards and poultry. When vineyards got diseased, the owners sent for Peter and he came and prayed and went up and down the vines saying, "You foul disease. I claim in the name of Jesus this field." Poultry houses developing fowl pest, that is as bad as foot and mouth in cattle. And he went to the poultry houses saying, "You foul pest. In the name of Jesus, get off this farm." I have eaten the fruit from the trees he has healed— better fruit than they ever had before. And he was a used car dealer, that was all, and he was a real man's man. A real man. That is the kind of manhood that is needed. Well, he just got filled with the power of the Spirit. He feared God, constantly used the name of Jesus, used the power of the Spirit.

And there is a fourth and last motive, love of the brethren. You will never make it on your own. If you are going to be a man of God, you will need brethren who love you — who love you enough that whatever you tell them doesn't break the relationship, doesn't stop them loving you. I have got a few men around the country like that and I value them highly. Fear of God, name of Jesus, power of the Spirit, love of the brethren—that's the motivation. A men's discipling group has got to introduce men to all those four things. That's quite an agenda, isn't it? Responsibility for yourself, your family, your church, your society, and those four motivations. You have got time when you're meeting once a month. You don't need to do it all in the first meeting. But there's an agenda for you, to produce men for God. That is where I am going to finish.

When teaching men I have prayed:

Father, I have done a lot of talking to my brothers. I pray first of all that if anything I have said is not the truth and not what you wanted said, would you please blot it out from their memories before it does any damage or causes them distraction. If I have been speaking from your heart, will your Holy Spirit so confirm it in their hearts that they know it was not me saying it but you. So they won't be talking about me but talking about you. Thank you, Lord, for their patience with me and for spending this time and I pray that their families may benefit from the time away from them, that when we go back to our loved ones that somehow they may sense that the time we have spent has been worthwhile and that we are better men for it.

Now Lord, I pray for the churches represented here. You know my heart, my longing, that in each of those churches they should do what the Lord Jesus did and disciple men, but I pray that you'll lay this on their hearts yourself so that they won't feel any pressure from me or anyone else but rather feel pressure from you to do this, however hard it may be, whatever may be necessary to see it through. Lord, I pray for that.

Finally, I pray that in the day when we see Jesus back here again, that not one may be missing on that day. Lord, keep us close to yourself. May we see it through, knowing that he who endures to the end shall be saved, and we look forward to that day and we long for it.

Even so, come Lord Jesus. You are the only hope for this world. In Jesus' name. Amen.

9 781913 472207